Parenting Your LGBTQ+ Teen

Parenting Your LGBTQ+ Teen

A Guide to Supporting, Empowering, and Connecting with Your Child

Allan Sadac, MBA, LMFT

ROCKRIDGE PRESS

For general information on our other products and services or to obtain technical support, please contact our Customer Care Department within the United States at (866) 744-2665, or outside the United States at (510) 253-0500.

Rockridge Press publishes its books in a variety of electronic and print formats. Some content that appears in print may not be available in electronic books, and vice versa.

Interior and Cover Designer: Mando Daniel
Art Producer: Sara Feinstein
Editor: Nora Spiegel
Production Editor: Matthew Burnett
Production Manager: Riley Hoffman

Author photograph courtesy of Aaron Jay Young.

Paperback ISBN: 978-1-64876-733-3
eBook ISBN: 978-1-64876-873-6

R2

This book is dedicated to all the biological parents, foster parents, adoptive parents, and other parental figures who are cheering on their LGBTQ+ children and teens.

Contents

Introduction

I came out when I was a sophomore at UC Davis in the 1990s. The first person I came out to in my family was my younger sister, Ann. It was not until my junior year that I was confronted by my mother. I can still remember that moment of shock, hearing my mother's voice over the phone: "Is it true? Is it true you are gay?" Let's just say the conversation did not go well. I had at that moment turned my mother's world upside down, and mine, too, and I knew things would never be the same again. For the next year, we barely spoke. But that cliché "time heals all wounds" luckily turned out to be true. It took several more years, but things got better over time. We continued to have our arguments and disagreements, but we got better at dealing with them. There were periods of time when we did not speak to one another, but eventually one of us would come around to initiate an awkward reconnection. We had to do the hard work, both individually and as a family, and eventually we figured it out. Wherever you may be in your journey with your teen, I am confident you will figure it out, too, and I hope the exercises, tips, real-life stories, and encouraging quotes in this book will give you guidance and empowerment through your journey.

As a licensed marriage and family therapist since 2001, I have met with many parents who either suspect or have learned their child or teen identifies as gay, lesbian, bisexual, or transgender (and other identifiers—more on that later). Every family is different, and their responses are different, but many feel powerless, confused, and scared. I am writing this book for parents like them, and for parents like you, who are seeking help and guidance to better support the children they love. Know that you are not alone; many people around the world are dealing with the same challenges you are. This book will help you figure out your path forward.

I assume you decided to pick up this book because you needed some guidance on how to best maneuver uncharted territory. You might be struggling or feeling stuck. Parenting an LGBTQ+ teen does require some different skills and knowledge, and I am here to help guide you. I recognize I am not going to be able to address or answer all the unique challenges my readers are faced with, but my hope is this is a helpful starting point for you to learn about what it means to be an LGBTQ+ teen today, and to get a handle on the best practices for supporting your teen as they navigate a crucial life transition. This may all be new to you, so take your time. I commend you for taking the important first step of picking up this book. You are on your way to knowing how to tackle parenting challenges, feeling better about yourself and how you parent, and gaining the confidence and tools you need to support your teen.

Please note that while using this book is a great way to work through feelings of low self-esteem or frustration, if you or your teen are dealing with any ongoing or debilitating feelings of depression, anxiety, or any other mental health issues, I encourage you to seek out professional help. If you are faced with parenting challenges that feel overwhelming or dangerous to you or other family members, or if you are unclear how to best care for your LGBTQ+ teen, it may be wise to consult a professional. This book is not meant to be a replacement for therapy, psychotropic medications, or medical treatment. There is no shame in seeking help or treatment.

Parenting is hard, and parenting an LGBTQ+ teen can present additional challenges. You must be willing to put in the work, face your fears about parenting, and be honest with yourselves about what you want for your family and your teen. I am confident this book will help you get there, and I am cheering you on as you embark on this precious, important, and rewarding work of supporting your LGBTQ+ teen so they—and you—may live your fullest life.

"There is no such thing as a perfect parent. So just be a real one."

—*Sue Atkins*

PART I

An Introduction to Parenting LGBTQ+ Teens

In part 1, we will establish some key parenting fundamentals and LGBTQ+ terminology, including what it means to be a parent, why raising teens is so tricky, what exactly *LGBTQ+* means, and what may be in store for your LGBTQ+ teen. These first couple chapters will prompt you to begin thinking about how you can better connect with your teen and create a meaningful relationship that affirms their queer identity. Coming out is also a journey for you—the parent—and self-reflecting and better understanding how to cultivate a loving and affirming connection with your teen can support your journey.

"Parents can only give good advice or put them on the right paths, but the final forming of a person's character lies in their own hands."

—*Anne Frank*

CHAPTER ONE

Parenting Teens 101

In this chapter, we'll talk about your role as a parent and
provide you with information to help you better understand, communicate, and connect with your LGBTQ+
teenager. Many parents struggle after their child comes
out because they fear they will say or do the wrong
thing. It can be intimidating when you have no idea what
worries, fears, and obstacles your LGBTQ+ teen is facing.
By the end of this chapter, I hope you can begin to feel
like you have some tools that you can immediately
benefit from. Also, by learning some LGBTQ+ terminology and concepts, you can show your teen that you are
trying and you want to connect to their heart.

Genesis and Tamika

Genesis is an 18-year-old high school senior. During a recent
holiday, she came out to her mother, Tamika, as a lesbian, and
shared that she has been dating a girl from school and would like
to invite her over to join the family for dinner. Tamika is struggling
with how to cope with the news. She is surprised at her conflicted
reaction, as she has LGBTQ+ friends and coworkers and has
never had a problem with sexual and gender diversity before.
Tamika loves her daughter and they have always had a close
relationship, but she does not know yet what Genesis's coming
out means to her.

Tamika and Genesis continue to be on cordial speaking terms, but it is still awkward between the two of them. Genesis repeatedly asks her mother if she has given any more thought about having her girlfriend at the house. Tamika has spoken with her close friend and a couple of carefully selected family members about what to do and how she can support Genesis. After a couple of months, Tamika finally, reluctantly agrees to meet Genesis's girlfriend. Tamika tells her daughter she is nervous, but she is ready. Tamika fears she will say or do something to upset Genesis and her girlfriend. She asks her daughter to be patient with her, tells her she is trying her best, and admits there is still so much she is trying to think through. The meeting is a start, but Tamika and Genesis know it will take more conversations and time.

What Does It Mean to Be a Parent?

Defining what it means to be a parent is not an easy thing to do. Being a parent is multilayered and can be defined relationally, generationally, individually, and by cultural norms. Some of you may not be a biological parent, but an extended biological family member who has stepped in, such as a grandparent, aunt, or uncle. You might be a foster parent, adoptive parent, or a group home provider. Parents and parental figures support a teen in developing their own values, as well as a healthy sense of self, security, responsibility, and confidence, to prepare them for their life as an adult. Being a parent means providing protection, respect, and other basic needs to support a child's healthy development of self throughout all their development years. It means being there for your teen, even when you might not agree with or understand their decisions. Being a parent can also mean grappling with complex feelings about how to keep your teen safe and protect them from hardships. It can also mean sadness or grief about particular hopes or dreams you had for your teen, which their sexual orientation or gender identity may now throw into question.

WHAT PARENTING ISN'T

There will be times when you will feel as if your teen is being outright defiant, disrespectful, or misguided. Despite these types of behaviors, you can still redirect them and set firm boundaries in a loving and caring way, without shaming them for who they are or using harmful punishments. On the flip side, sometimes parents can blur the lines by being too lenient, causing their teens to see them more as friends than as parents. I encourage you to find ways to let your LGBTQ+ teen know there are rules and boundaries and that you still love them.

You've Made It Through the First 12 Years. Now What?

This can be a very scary and worrisome time for you as a parent. You may feel as though you have no idea how to raise a teen and have no idea what their coming out means for you and your family. Your teen might be spending more time outside of your home or isolating in their room. Perhaps the hormones of puberty are wreaking havoc, and every time you reach out it results in an argument.

A great place to start is to talk to your teenager and try your best to just listen to them, without judgment. It is amazing how much you can learn if you just leave your ego, your insecurities, and your anger aside and take the time to absorb what your teenager is willing to share. Being patient with yourself and your teenager is also critical. It is important to remember your unconditional support and availability is what you both need. Simply take the time to show up for your LGBTQ+ teen every day and stay open to learning. You have been there for the first 12 years; now your job is to continue to show up for them.

The Teenage Years Force You to Rethink Your Role as a Parent

One of the biggest challenges I see in my practice is parents who have not made effective changes along with the changing developmental stages of their child. Being the parent of a teenager requires a different skill set than being a parent of a seven-year-old. I know that sometimes it feels as if you're going crazy because you're trying to figure out what your teen needs by paying close attention to their verbal and nonverbal communications. What might their actions be trying to tell you? What are they not saying out loud? Just like you, they might not always know how to best communicate or even know what is troubling them, but everything they do is telling you something.

Remember that during the teenage years, your teenager is trying to figure out who they are. They might not be coming to you as much as you would like or as much as they did when they were younger. One of the most loving things a parent can do is give their teenager the space to learn how to problem-solve on their own and to think critically about challenges they are facing every day.

YOUR TEEN IS ALSO RETHINKING THE ROLE OF THE CHILD

Your teenager may seem as though they are all over the place. They are erratic and impulsive, and all you want is for them to think things through. Your teen more than likely has been feeling insecure and unsure about themself, wondering how to fit in and how to respond to expectations from you, friends, teachers, other family members, and society as a whole. They do not want to feel as if they are disappointing those important to them. Your job is to reinforce self-confidence, self-esteem, self-nurturance, self-empathy, and self-acceptance so they can gain clarity about who they want to become.

QUIZ: WHAT IS YOUR PARENTING STYLE?

How you choose to parent will have a significant impact on how your teen develops and grows into adulthood, and will influence how comfortable your teen feels about coming to you for advice and support when they need it. If your goal is to understand and have a closer relationship with your teen, then it would be helpful to figure out how to embrace a parenting style that encourages a healthier parent–teen relationship.

With which of the following statements do you most identify?

Authoritarian

☐ My teen should do what I say because I said so.

☐ I yell at my teen to let them know they have misbehaved.

☐ I criticize my kid to improve their behavior.

☐ When I'm mad at my teen, I withhold my love.

☐ I use threats to control their behavior.

Authoritative

☐ I am responsive to my teen's needs.

☐ I consider my teen's opinion.

☐ I acknowledge my teen's good behaviors and successes.

☐ I explain myself to my teen.

☐ I am a warm and loving parent.

Permissive

- ☐ I bribe my kid with material things or food.
- ☐ I don't often enforce rules.
- ☐ When my teen whines or complains, I just give in to their request.
- ☐ We don't have much structure or a schedule.
- ☐ My teen is my best friend.

Uninvolved

- ☐ I have my own problems to deal with.
- ☐ My teen is old enough to manage things on their own.
- ☐ I have very little or no behavioral expectations.
- ☐ I'm not the warm and affectionate kind of parent.
- ☐ I often miss school events and other occasions.

If you most identified with the authoritarian, permissive, or uninvolved parenting styles, think about how those styles may be affecting your relationship with your teen. I encourage you to consider shifting to a more authoritative style. Embracing authoritative parenting methods will help you strengthen your relationship with your LGBTQ+ teen and support their growing autonomy.

Adolescence Defined

Adolescence is defined as the age range between 10 and 21 years old, and is a time of profound physical, emotional, social, mental, and psychological growth and development. It is the age when all individuals strive to find a healthy development of their identity, self-esteem, social and emotional well-being, and social acceptance. This developmental stage can be particularly difficult for LGBTQ+ teens because of the added level of sensitivity and vulnerability that comes with feeling different. This is the period of development when your teen is noticing they are (or aren't) starting to develop romantic attractions to their peers, which can bring up fear and overwhelming worry about what their family and friends would think of their physical and emotional attraction to their same-sex peers. Depending on where you live and the local attitudes, this is a time when some LGBTQ+ teens might develop challenges with depression and anxiety due to an overwhelming fear of being teased, bullied, or physically and verbally abused. This is also a critical period because it is when secondary sexual organs develop, and for some this is accompanied by gender incongruence or gender dysphoria, which is when there is a mental and physical mismatch between parts of one's anatomy that are typically gendered and how one sees themself.

THE STAGES OF ADOLESCENCE

There are three primary stages of adolescence: early, middle, and late. The early stage (ages 10 to 13) is when puberty begins, and this is often the time when individuals begin to wonder about their gender identity and sexual orientation. Middle adolescence (ages 14 to 17) is when teens are inquisitive about romantic and sexual experiences, in addition to their values, beliefs, and identity. Late adolescence (ages 18 to 21) is when a teen's identity, including their romantic and sexual interests, are more developed, and they feel more settled with their individuality, without seeking the approval of others as much.

Why Is Parenting Teens So Hard?

Parenting adolescents is an exceptionally difficult time for many parents, for many different reasons. As a teen grows physically, starts spending more time with friends, and wants to make more of their own decisions, parents often experience a loss of their child, who was so closely attached to and dependent on them. A parent may not know how to cope with their child's assertions of independence as they try to figure out who they are and who they want to be on their way to becoming a young adult.

Another reason parenting teens is so hard is the seemingly constant emotional volatility and dizzying shifts of their self-expression, physical appearance, social pressures, interests, values, opinions, peer groups, and for some, gender identity and sexual orientation. It can be hard for parents to allow their teen some space to try on different figurative hats and make mistakes from which they can learn and grow. As hard as it may be, do your best to remain calm, listen to your teen, and continue to be available to support them through their journey toward young adulthood.

THEY ARE BECOMING MORE INDEPENDENT

Think of adolescence as a time for your teen to practice and learn to be more independent. It can be very difficult for parents to balance having boundaries with also giving their teens some leeway and letting them learn how to think on their feet, take responsibility for their decisions, and come up with their own solutions. This will require you to be patient on the sidelines and to know when to step in. This balancing act is a skill where practice makes better (and rarely, if ever, perfect).

THEY ARE PHYSICALLY GROWING AND CHANGING

For LGBTQ+ teens, the physical and developmental changes during adolescence can bring up difficulties with sexual identity, especially for those who are wondering if they might be a different gender than they were assigned at birth. Additionally, teens discover their bodies respond to their sexual and romantic attractions, and sometimes they have little control over these reactions. They begin noticing and comparing themselves to others in the locker room, and they overhear conversations of sexual activity and curiosities from their peers. Their brain development is also creating new neural pathways, affecting their worldviews and emotional reactions, and most important, helping develop their cause-and-effect thinking skills.

THEY ARE MAKING THEIR OWN DECISIONS

LGBTQ+ teens are trying to exercise their independence by making their own decisions about their lives, who they are, who they want to be, what they want to do, and which people they want to surround themselves with. It is important for parents to recognize the advantages of allowing their teen to make their own decisions and learn from the consequences of their decisions. Teens grow in confidence and resilience when they can fall sometimes and learn they can pick themselves back up.

THEY DON'T NEED YOU AS MUCH AS THEY USED TO

This is a time in your teen's development when you will probably feel less needed. Rather than worrying about it, remember that your teenager is preparing for young adulthood and learning how to problem-solve, develop self-confidence, and figure out who they are and what they want. The reality is that your teen still needs you—it just might look different than what you were expecting. Let them know you are still there for them no matter what and create an affirming environment for their LGBTQ+ identity, and they will continue to come to you when they need your support and guidance.

Interesting Statistics on Teens Today

Just as in past generations, the teens of today are different from the ones who came before them. Advances in mobile technology in recent years have introduced changes and exacerbated some challenges of being a teen. Teenagers today spend a considerable amount of time staring at screens (smartphones, televisions, tablets, computers, and laptops), so much so that many report inadequate sleep due to excessive use of electronic gadgets. Some reports suggest an average of more than nine hours of screen time daily.

More teenagers are reporting their primary social connections are virtual rather than in person. They are flooded with photographs of peers doing fun things, sometimes fads that are unsafe, and report experiencing FOMO (fear of missing out), slut-shaming, and other forms of online bullying. This has resulted in more teens reporting feelings such as anxiety and depression. Data from the Pew Research Center indicates an approximate 8 percent increase in depression among teens from 10 years ago. In addition to challenges with communication, socialization, and healthy relationships—skills best learned through face-to-face interactions—teenagers today deal with issues of online privacy because of the sharing of nude selfies, easier visibility of unsolicited sexual material, and sexting.

On the bright side, contemporary teenagers are also more open to gender-nonconforming identities and are more likely to interact with peers who identify as LGBTQ+. Overall, teens today are more interested in politics and the role of government in solving problems, about 35 percent know someone who uses gender-neutral pronouns, 48 percent are nonwhite, and 45 percent of those eligible voted in the 2020 US presidential election. There is more racial diversity among teens today, and according to a May 2021 Gallup poll, 84 percent of young adults support same-sex marriage.

Our Modern World Is Turning Kids into Teens Quicker Than Ever Before

Today's teens are being exposed to mature realities at a younger age than ever before. With the click of a mouse or a swipe on a smartphone, teens are exposed to the latest fads, celebrity gossip, and news—from varying levels of reputable sources. They are watching videos and reading about romantic relationships and sex—including having access to porn. In addition, teens are being exposed to pressures of drugs, alcohol, and sex at a younger age. LGBTQ+ teens are consistently being exposed to many new things before their minds are ready and sufficiently developed to wisely deal with them.

A MINDFULNESS MEDITATION FOR CHALLENGING TIMES

Meditation is a way we can find peace in the present moment and return to ourselves. It can be an incredible resource in times of stress, or as a regular practice. Just taking a little bit of time for this important form of self-care can fortify you to deal with your challenges (including parenting) with greater calm and clarity. The following is a simple mindfulness meditation that can be practiced at any time.

1. Find yourself a quiet place without distractions. You can even put up a "Do Not Disturb" sign on the door.

2. Get into a comfortable position, such as sitting cross-legged on cushions on the floor, upright in a comfortable chair, or lying down on your bed.

3. Set a timer for however long you want. Five minutes might be a good start until you get the hang of it. Take a few deep breaths in through your nose, then exhale out through your mouth.

4. After a few deep breaths, breathe as you normally would. With every inhale, think of things that bring you calm and relaxation (e.g., your favorite beach or place in nature). With every exhale, imagine releasing whatever stressor(s) you are facing.

5. It is natural for your thoughts to wander. Acknowledge the intruding thoughts without judgment, then try to focus on the moment, also without judgment. What are you feeling? Where are you feeling it in your body? What do you smell?

6. When the timer goes off, slowly open your eyes and bring yourself back.

CELL PHONES AND SOCIAL MEDIA

Teens are seeking places where they feel acceptance and can be themselves, and for many LGBTQ+ teens, especially those living in rural and small communities, their cell phones and social media outlets are their only access to the LGBTQ+ community and the support and information they need to feel affirmed. Cell phones and social media do carry risks (sexting, cyberbullying, sharing provocative selfies, and online predators), so it is important to have conversations with your teen about safety and how they can protect themself when using these types of technology.

NEWS, MEDIA, AND INFORMATION OVERLOAD

The abundance of news and media outlets these days can be overwhelming for today's LGBTQ+ teens. Young people have shared with me unsettling anxiety and fear because of nonstop news, alerts, and notifications of civil unrest, political fights, racial strife, and various types of hate crimes. Check in with your teen about how they can better manage their media consumption to avoid information overload, and teach them basic media literacy skills so they can make sure they're getting their information from reliable and reputable sources. Think about how you are modeling for your teen with your own media consumption.

THE HARSH REALITIES OF THE WORLD

LGBTQ+ teens can be at risk of various types of hardships, such as bullying, not only online, but also in different social and familial settings. It is important for you as a parent to check in with your teen and ask them if they feel safe at school and in the community. Make sure they know you will help them when they don't feel they can stand up for themself. Though your teen is growing more independent, it is still your job as a parent to protect them from harmful situations.

AN IMMENSE PRESSURE TO SUCCEED

LGBTQ+ teens are no different than most other teens as they try to figure out how to feel successful and happy about themselves. No matter where they fall in the acronym, there are plenty of social pressures, influences, competitions, and expectations imposed on them. These may be external or self-imposed pressures based on grades or academic performance, or these may be expectations driven by a sense of inadequacy because of their sexual orientation and gender identity. Encourage your teen to be their best version of themself in their own way.

Actions Speak Louder Than Words

Seeing is believing. Often the best way to show your teenager you are open and accepting is through your actions. You can communicate this to your LGBTQ+ teen by doing some of the following:

- Encourage your teen to have friends over at your home.
- Sit down and express interest in talking about the topics and activities your teenager is interested in.
- Maximize opportunities when you can share your involvement with LGBTQ+ groups like PFLAG (Parents, Family, and Friends of Lesbians and Gays).
- Show your teen you are a supporter in the way you speak positively about LGBTQ+ subjects with your friends and family.
- Take time to learn about LGBTQ+ culture, important icons, and role models from the queer community.
- Go to a gay pride event with your teenager.
- Sit next to them, hold their hand, or give them a hug. Look at them and smile. Tell them you're proud of them.
- Do the same things you did before they came out to you.

Teenagers Are Just Trying to Find Their Way through an Increasingly Complex World

One day you are considered a child, and then, before you know it, you are thrust into the complicated topography of adolescent life without an instruction manual. Life used to be so simple without these new social and academic pressures. Your teen once knew exactly where they stood and how they were supposed to behave, feeling safe and confident within their family bubble. But then LGBTQ+ teens begin to be more conscious of being "cool" as they grow up, constantly vacillating between wanting to stay close to the nest and wanting to assert independence and self-sufficiency. Teens begin to notice changes in their bodies, and in how others are noticing those bodily changes. They begin to be confronted with situations and challenges they did not have to deal with before, such as formulating opinions about social, environmental, and political issues. They may feel conflicted about choosing between loyalty to familiar friends they have had since kindergarten and a desire to make new friends who are in a different crowd. Teens are also experimenting and making a lot of new discoveries about the values that are important to them. They simultaneously want the protection and simplicity of childhood, while also yearning to be grown-ups who can make independent decisions—not an easy place to be for any teenager.

I Don't Wanna Talk About It

As teenagers get older, they want to deal with things on their own. They don't want to talk to their parents, often out of fear of being reprimanded or judged. It is normal for teens to feel more comfortable talking to their peers, but this does not mean they don't need the support of their parents. Here is an example of how you can handle these types of situations and let your teen know you are still there for them.

Parent: I got a call today from your school. I heard you had some problems with some of the kids at school. I'd like to hear from you what happened.

Teen: I didn't do anything wrong.

Parent: I don't think you did anything wrong.

Teen: I don't wanna talk about it.

Parent: I hope you know I am here to listen any time. I hear you don't want to talk about it, but is there anything I can do to help?

Teen: Yeah, you can stop making a big deal about it. I just want to forget today.

Parent: Okay, well, I love you and I just want to help. If you change your mind, I will be in the living room. I'm here for you any time.

Teen: (no verbal response)

As a parent, it can be hard to know when (and how) to help and when to give your child space. You can feel helpless, ineffective, or rejected when your efforts are declined. Remember that simply acknowledging your teen and letting them know you are available, if and when they are ready, is being supportive.

LGBTQ+ Teens Face an Even More Complicated Path

Despite what might look like an improved social openness and acceptance of the LGBTQ+ community—increased acceptance of gay marriage, more LGBTQ+ athletes and celebrities, and more political allies—LGBTQ+ teens are still a minority. LGBTQ+ individuals of color often report an added level of prejudice, unfair treatment, and higher levels of bullying and verbal attacks. The reality is that there is still so much we must learn as a society to improve our cultural competence and understanding.

Certain politicians and political parties are intent on infringing on the rights of LGBTQ+ people, encouraging discriminatory policies, and establishing roadblocks to accessing critical government and health services. There are still parts of the country that have laws against teachers and staff speaking about LGBTQ+ issues in school, and sex education in schools is still predominantly taught from a heteronormative viewpoint. (Heteronormativity is the notion or opinion that all people are heterosexual, or assuming heterosexuality is the "normal" state of human sexuality and gender identity.) Even when LGBTQ+ teens are raised in supportive families and communities, they are still bombarded with hostility and messaging that they are inferior.

Your Job Is to Encourage and Guide Them

No matter what you think or how you feel about your LGBTQ+ teen's sexual and/or gender identity, it is critical for you to be the anchor for safety, security, and compassion for your child. Think about your own teen years and try to remember what it was like for you, and know this is an even more challenging period for your LGBTQ+ teen. They need to know there is someone looking out for them, someone who is walking alongside them every step of the way.

Your teen is going to make mistakes. They will make errors in judgment about who to be friends with and perhaps who they come out to. They will have struggles in their relationships, not know how to handle strong feelings, face challenges at school, and make difficult decisions about sex. They will need you to let them make their mistakes and still be there to pick them up when they do. Allow them the space to come to you, and show them in subtle ways you are always available to them.

This Book Will Show You How

In this chapter, it was my goal to get you to reexamine your role as a parent, but please know that this does not in any way mean I think you are a bad parent. I have the utmost faith and confidence that you love your child, want the best for them, and have been dealing the best way you know how. I encourage you to try some new and different ways to parent and to be more effective as a guide, supporter, teacher, and loving protector of your LGBTQ+ teen.

It is never easy to look at yourself and to step out of your comfort zone. But being a parent demands you do what is necessary in order to support the development and growth of your teen. Parenting is not one-size-fits-all, and it requires you know which unique strengths and tools are going to reach your teen. Your involvement as a parent continues to be a key factor in your child's success, and I trust that the tools you learn in this book will help you on your way to becoming the parent you yearn to be.

Conclusion

Now that we have covered some basics about parenting and LGBTQ+ teens, the next chapter will delve deeper into more specific elements of parenting and further expand your understanding of the LGBTQ+ experience. The more you learn, the more you can understand yourself and your teen's sexual orientation and gender identity. Even with all the progress we have made socially, there are still huge gaps in what we know and what we think we know about the LGBTQ+ community.

As a reminder, take whatever time you need to digest the information from the first chapter and figure out how it fits your needs. Take time to reread sections, make note of questions, and let your curiosity wander. I want this book to be a source of inspiration for you as well as a source of answers to your questions. Stick with me and allow me to help you further.

"If I wait for someone else to validate my existence, it will mean that I'm shortchanging myself."

—*Zanele Muholi*

CHAPTER TWO

What Does It Mean to Be an LGBTQ+ Teen?

Many parents do not know where the *LGBTQ+* acronym came from, much less what the different letters and identities mean. This chapter will cover the acronym, focusing on a range of sexual orientations and gender identities as they relate to adolescence. I will also begin to talk about the different challenges today's LGBTQ+ teens face. Keep in mind that your teen's sexual identity and gender identity are still developing. Your support throughout this process will make it easier for your teen to gain clarity through healthy experimentation and self-exploration. It is my hope that having a broad understanding of the range of struggles your teen could be facing will help you figure out how to support them. I also want to continue to focus on furthering your self-awareness and knowledge, so that you may increase your confidence and knowledge of available tools to better support your teen.

Gabriel

Meet Gabriel, a 14-year-old gay male who lives in a farming community with a population of about 75,000 people. Gabriel lives with his mother, stepfather, stepbrother, and younger sister. Starting in seventh grade, he has been feeling and seeing himself differently from his peers, often worrying there is something wrong with him, but he just doesn't quite know what it is. At first, these thoughts came on infrequently, but as of late, they seem to get louder and louder.

Gabriel tries very hard to act according to and adopt the heteronormative beliefs and expectations that his family, friends, and society place on him. He is intelligent and well-liked among most of his peers. But he is increasingly feeling conflicted because he knows he is supposed to like girls, but instead the people who predominantly catch his attention are the other boys, especially during gym class. Gabriel spends many moments throughout the school day anxious that he isn't acting right, wondering what is wrong with him. He has thoughts of doing things with other boys and feels immense shame about it.

Gabriel's mother has noticed Gabriel acting differently but cannot seem to pinpoint what has changed. She has been introducing Gabriel to her friends' daughters and often makes jokes about Gabriel maybe dating one of them, but Gabriel just laughs it off. Gabriel's mother is shocked he hasn't been interested in dating, and he seems to always find an excuse to avoid the conversation. Gabriel's mother suspects her son might be gay, but she is afraid of asking and offending him.

Your Child Will Always Be Evolving and Changing

Hang on, because you are in for a bumpy ride. Your teenager has left the starting gates of adolescence, and you might be feeling lost and overwhelmed. Things are moving much too fast as you try to keep up and stay in control. For your teen, on the other hand, things aren't moving fast enough. Your teenager is developing, transforming, and preparing to be an independent adult. They are racing to get to the finish line called adulthood the best way they know how. I encourage you to hold on and have faith that it will all work out in the end. You cannot control every change your teen goes through, but you can walk beside them. Consider the fact that, no matter what your intentions, you are constantly communicating to your teenager how you feel and how you think about them through your body language and facial expressions—even when you're saying nothing. Ask yourself what messages you are giving your teenager and be aware that your messages may leave a lasting influence.

It's Your Job to Support Them, Not Dictate Who They Become

You are trying hard to be a good parent, and you think your efforts to advise and guide your LGBTQ+ teen are well-intentioned. But know when teens grow up in an environment where their opinions and thoughts are not valued, their self-esteem tends to be compromised. Being constantly dictated to and told who you should be instills a sense of powerlessness. When young people are unable to be their true selves, they risk developing feelings of self-hatred, turning anger, fear, resentment, and hostility inward. Overwhelming feelings of sadness and anxiety become the focus, instead of more productive and character-building goals. If your teen feels their voice is being silenced, they will continue to hide who they really are, rather than learning to accept and express themself with confidence.

Consider adolescence as a time for your teen to explore and experiment with who they want to be. Supporting them, even when it's hard for you, validates and strengthens their character and facilitates their evolution.

His Name Is Gab

The following example of a mother and her transgender son at a family gathering illustrates a common experience of many parents and their trans teenagers.

Aunt: Hi, Gabriella, how are you? Oh my, why are you dressed like that? People might mistake you for a boy.

Teen: I'm fine, Auntie. (*Puts head down, avoiding making eye contact.*)

Parent: Gab is fine. He is doing well at school and has started exploring some new interests.

Aunt: That is great. I am glad things are going well at school. You know, I almost forgot that your cousin Jennifer has some clothes she has grown out of. I'll make sure to send them with you before you leave today.

Parent: Oh, that won't be necessary. Gab has enough clothes that he likes just fine.

Aunt: I see.

Parent: You know, Sis, Gab and I would really appreciate it if you called him by his name. His name is Gab and his pronouns are he/him. It's how my son wants to be called.

Aunt: But, Gabriella . . .

Parent: No buts. You know family is really important, and Gab loves his cousins, which is why we are here. But I really need for you to respect my son and how he wants to be called. My son means the world to me and I stand with him. I hope you can respect our wishes. (*Parent looks at Gab and smiles.*)

Aunt: Okay, Gab. I'm sorry. I'm still getting used to all the changes.

Teen: Thanks, Auntie. (*Turns to parent, hugs her.*) Thanks, Mom.

Relationships with extended family can be hard, and it can be especially hard for many transgender teens to stand up for themselves. Seeing you stand up for them and support them helps your teen learn they can stand up for themself and lets them know you have their back.

What Does It Mean to Be LGBTQ+?

The acronym *LGBTQ+* is a spectrum of different sexual and gender identities. *LGBTQ+* stands for lesbian, gay, bisexual, transgender, questioning or queer, and the "+" is for other orientations and gender identities. If you are finding it a bit confusing, that's okay. To be honest, it can even be difficult for those of us who are part of the community of letters!

In the 1990s this acronym was shorter, simply *GLBT*, and it included gays, lesbians, bisexuals, and transgender people. Around the mid-2000s, in response to perceived misogyny within the queer community, there was concern that lesbians were being minimized, and so "LGBT" became the new sequence of letters. The acronym has grown as we have gotten better at understanding the expansive fluidity of sexuality. The range of different identities is now often associated with other terms such as *gender expression, sex assigned at birth,* and *sexual and romantic orientation.*

The following details about each of the letters will not only help clarify your understanding of the different orientations and gender identities, but I also hope it will highlight the expansive variations your teen is trying to figure out for themself. It is also worth noting that one's sexual orientation and gender identity are not set in stone. It is not unusual for LGBTQ+ individuals to experiment and experience them in evolving ways. It is very important you remain curious and open-minded, knowing your child will always be the person most qualified to define themself.

LESBIAN

The orientation label known as *lesbian* has been around for well over 100 years, and it is the term used when a woman or nonbinary person is romantically, sexually, and/or physically attracted to other women and nonbinary people. Lesbians choose to express themselves in different ways, ranging from socially defined feminine expressions (femme) to more masculine expressions (butch), and there are also transgender people who identify as lesbian (remember, gender identity and sexual orientation are separate things). It is generally good practice to ask how someone identifies, as it is not uncommon for women to have same-gender experiences and feelings but to not identify as lesbian.

GAY

Since as early as the 1920s, the term *gay* has historically been an umbrella term used for anyone who is not heterosexual, though in this context it means a man or nonbinary person who is sexually, physically, and/or romantically attracted to other men and nonbinary people. *Gay* has become the preferred term compared to *homosexual,* and is a word often associated with and used by people of all genders. Some gay men take on more socially defined feminine interests and characteristics, while others maintain a more masculine expression. Like other orientations, not all men who have sexual, physical, and/or emotional experiences with other men identify as gay.

BISEXUAL

A bisexual individual is sexually, physically, and romantically attracted to two or more genders. Some people prefer the term *pansexual*, meaning that they are attracted to all genders or regardless of gender. There are some, even within the LGBTQ+ community, who refuse to believe anyone is truly bisexual. Biphobia and prejudice toward this group is very present within the LGBTQ+ community, and bisexual people, especially men, are often told they are "confused" or "can't decide." Bisexuals can feel isolated because they do not completely identify as gay or lesbian.

TRANSGENDER

A transgender individual is a person whose gender identity does not match the gender they were assigned at birth. A transgender person might identify as binary, meaning they identify as exclusively a man or a woman; or there are also nonbinary individuals who could feel like a mix of genders, like their gender is fluid, or like they have no gender at all. Transgender teens often struggle with how they see themselves in relation to the genitalia they were born with. They are also most susceptible to threat, physical and sexual assault, and verbal abuse—particularly if they are also people of color. Transgender people often endure many years of struggles before they can socially and/or medically transition and have the markers on their driver's license to match their gender identity. However, not all transgender people seek to medically transition. Recent advances in medicine have made it an option for some teens who are questioning their gender identity to hit a biological pause button, thanks to medications known as puberty blockers and hormone blockers. Although still controversial, there has been significant support for and success with these treatments. There are no long-term negative effects from the use of puberty blockers and they are even used for cisgender teens who develop too early.

QUEER OR QUESTIONING

Q stands for queer and is generally associated with individuals whose orientation and identity are not heterosexual or cisgender (someone whose gender identity corresponds with their sex assigned at birth). Historically, this term has been used in a hurtful and derogatory way, but in recent years, there has been an effort to reclaim this term and use it with a more positive and empowering spirit.

Q can also stand for questioning—individuals who are in a developmental stage in their life when they are unsure and are trying to figure out their sexual orientation and gender identity. Questioning is normal and natural, and may be where your teen finds themself for a while until they figure things out.

INTERSEX

Intersex is a broad term describing individuals whose physical and reproductive characteristics do not fall cleanly into the definition of "male" or "female." Intersex people are born with both female and male anatomy, physiology, and/or chromosomes; thus, the individual will often struggle into adolescence until they have a better idea of their gender identity and expression. It is still common for harmful surgery to be conducted on the genitalia of young intersex children to assign sex without their consent, but this practice is luckily losing favor and becoming outlawed in some states. Surgery conducted later in development once the intersex individual is old enough to say what their true gender identity is, or whether they want surgery at all, is more favorable. It's important to note that intersex people can be cisgender and straight, and there is still debate on whether intersex people should be considered LGBTQ+.

ASEXUAL

Asexual individuals (also referred to as "ace") experience a lack of sexual attraction and aromantic ("aro") individuals experience a lack of romantic attraction. However, asexuality and aromanticism exist on a spectrum, and some people may identify as grey-asexual or demisexual or gray-romantic, along with various other labels. Depending on where someone falls on the aro-ace spectrum, they may still want sexual or romantic attachments. Individuals in this category are often misunderstood and can experience an exceptionally difficult time managing in a sex- and romance-focused world.

PANSEXUAL

Pansexual is often used interchangeably and confused with *bisexual*. It typically implies a more equal attraction to various genders, whereas bisexuals might have preferences. Pansexuals are attracted either emotionally, physically, or both to all genders. The broad and comprehensive range of sexuality includes (but is not limited to) men, women, agender or genderfluid people, and nonbinary people in general.

GENDERQUEER

Genderqueer is a gender identity term similar to, but often confused with the term nonbinary. Genderqueer individuals describe themselves as neither female or male, both female and male, or varying degrees of female and male. They often reject social gender norms and restrictive labels. There is fluidity and freedom from having to fit into a mold of one's assigned gender, which supports a more authentic internal relationship between one's body and how they think about themself. For many genderqueer individuals, their gender identity and their gender expression can develop over the course of several years of self-discovery.

Important Statistics on LGBTQ+ Teens

Following are some current LGBTQ+ insights that will enhance your understanding your LGBTQ+ teen's world.

- In comparison to their heterosexual peers, LGBTQ+ teens are 2x more likely to experience being verbally harassed or called names at school.
- When LGBTQ+ teens were questioned about the most important current problem they are facing, the top three (from the highest to lowest percentages) were non-acceptance by their family, school-related problems (including bullying), and fear of being open or outed.
- 42% of LGBTQ+ teens reported thinking the community where they live is not accepting of those who identify as LGBTQ+.
- 73% of LGBTQ+ teens are more honest within their online environment than with people in the physical world.
- 1/3 of those interviewed reported not having any adult to talk to about their problems.
- LGBTQ+ teens are 4x more likely to attempt suicide.
- Compared to the other groups under the LGBTQ+ acronym, trans teens experience far greater levels of bullying and physical assault. 75% of transgender youth fear experiencing harm while at school.

These sobering statistics speak to the unique challenges and struggles LGBTQ+ teens are dealing with. Use this information to help yourself become more attentive to the potential red flags, and consider ways you might need to assist and show compassion for your teen.

Coming Out

Coming out is a personal decision that will change your LGBTQ+ teen's life forever. Coming out is not a one-time experience but a lifetime of individual choices. People often feel incredible anxiety, even agony, before deciding to come out to another person, wondering how the person will respond and perhaps fearing they could lose a family member, a friend, or their employment. Unlike their heterosexual and cisgender peers, your teen will have to come out repeatedly over the course of their lives to new friends, teachers, bosses, coworkers, and romantic interests. It is just a part of being LGBTQ+, and it does get easier over time. I encourage, as a parent, you to let your teen know how much it means to you they trusted you with such a huge part of who they are. Let them know how brave you think they are. Coming out is a tremendously courageous decision each and every time, no matter how many times one has done it before.

Terminology Is Constantly Evolving and Expanding

Over the decades, we have come to learn more and more about the diversity and nuances of the range of sexual orientation, sexuality, gender identity, and gender expression. Since the time I came out in the 1990s, tremendous amounts of new knowledge and information about LGBTQ+ individuals have become available. This body of knowledge is not static by any means, but instead continues to unfold and advance. I, too, am still learning, and I don't expect you as a parent to learn and know everything. But there is value in recognizing that we are *all* learning, and I offer this perspective to express my understanding and compassion for you and your efforts to be a better parent for your

LGBTQ+ teen. If parents can allow themselves to be humble and learn from their teens, it can be a wonderful way for parents and children to connect and bond together.

STAY CURRENT, STAY INFORMED

As a parent of an LGBTQ+ teen, I encourage you to do your best to keep up with LGBTQ+ trends, news, television shows, celebrities, and influencers. Having some knowledge and familiarity with your teenager's interests will not only allow you to find things you can talk about, but will also help you be more aware of the messages and information your teen is consuming. Your teen will also notice that you are trying and care enough to learn about their world, even if you might not completely understand or buy in to it.

■ A BREATHING EXERCISE

If you are feeling overwhelmed and anxious, one of the most helpful exercises you can do is to just breathe. An exercise I often teach patients is the 4-7-8 breathing technique created by Dr. Andrew Weil, which can be quite effective in helping shift an agitated or stressed mental and emotional state into a more relaxed and peaceful one. You don't need any equipment or props, and you can do it practically anywhere and anytime.

While sitting up comfortably with your back straight, do the following steps:

1. Start with a complete exhale through your mouth.

2. With your mouth closed, inhale through your nose for four seconds.

3. Now hold your breath for seven seconds.

4. Then exhale through your mouth for eight seconds.

5. Repeat steps 2 through 4 three more times, for a total of four cycles.

LGBTQ+ Teens Face
Unique Challenges

Growing up today is difficult for any teenager, but growing up while also dealing with LGBTQ+-related challenges is even more difficult, and in some instances even threatening. I do not mean to stir up the worries you already feel as a parent, but I do think it is important for us to be frank about issues with which your teen might need your guidance and support. Incidences of discrimination in both metropolitan and rural areas are higher for LGBTQ+ teenagers. LGBTQ+ teens are also at higher risk of mental illnesses such as PTSD, depression, and anxiety due to the social pressures and stigmas against being lesbian, gay, bisexual, transgender, or any other marginalized orientation or gender identity. These emotional and mental health challenges are even further escalated by a lack of support in schools, the community, and many times at home. I will continue to expand and examine other challenges in the following sections of this chapter.

DISCRIMINATION

Homophobia and transphobia continue to be a challenge for many LGBTQ+ teens, even in metropolitan, "progressive" communities. There continues to be anti-LGBTQ+ rhetoric on many levels of politics, including local school districts. Discrimination in various forms still pushes heteronormative and cisnormative biases onto LGBTQ+ teens and their parents. (Cisnormative is the notion or opinion that all people are cisgender, or the assumption that cisgender is the "normal" state of human gender identity.) Among medical professionals, there remains a lack of training in cultural LGBTQ+ sensitivity, particularly regarding healthcare for transgender and intersex individuals.

BODY ISSUES

Regardless of where a person falls in the LGBTQ+ acronym, looking and feeling positive about one's body is a challenging hurdle for LGBTQ+ teenagers. The saturation of gender-conforming standards of beauty pressure LGBTQ+ teens into believing they must look and behave a particular way in order to be desirable. Many LGBTQ+ teens suffer from eating disorders and body dysmorphia, bombarded by images telling them they must maintain a specific physique in order to be attractive. This is amplified even more in transgender teens, who are also struggling with understanding and expressing their gender identities.

LOW SELF-ESTEEM

Self-esteem is about the way your LGBTQ+ teen can recognize their value. A teenager with low self-esteem will find it very difficult to recognize their strengths and positive attributes. If you add in mental health issues such as depression or anxiety, this makes it even more difficult for a teen to be honest and realistic about themself and practice self-acceptance.

LACK OF CONFIDENCE

Even in some of the more progressive and accepting communities, there are still those who believe strongly that there is no place for LGBTQ+ teens. The constant negative and disempowering messaging LGBTQ+ teens receive on various social media platforms, from their teachers, communities, places of worship, and peers feeds into their lack of confidence. This is a critical issue that is often tied to risky decisions and poor academic performance.

LOW SELF-WORTH

Feeling worthy is tough when we live in a society that places so much value on the external and superficial: being well liked and accepted by peers, wearing the right clothes, and looking the part. Imagine being told every day from multiple sources that you are not normal and that God does not love you. These constant messages are difficult to ignore, even with the most resilient personality and characters.

LONELINESS/ISOLATION

Feeling alone and lonely is common for many LGBTQ+ teens, who also report higher percentages of depression and anxiety compared to their heterosexual peers. These emotions are further intensified by a lack of social and family support. As LGBTQ+ teens are already a minority in most environments, the isolation they may feel is further exacerbated in schools and communities where there are few other people who are out. LGBTQ+ teens often feel isolated in a world that does not accept them or want them in their schools, sports teams, churches, communities, and even—far too often—their own families.

SELF-LOATHING

LGBTQ+ teens often live with constant negative self-talk and loud cognitive distortions that feed their self-loathing. Their minds are bombarded with statements such as "I'm a freak," "I'm dumb," "I'm worthless," "No one loves me," "I don't want to go back to school and deal with those mean homophobic kids," "I'm a weirdo," and "Something is wrong with me." These are just some of the many painful thoughts that are so hard for many LGBTQ+ teens to silence.

❚ PEN AND PAPER

I often encourage my patients to do some form of journaling or freewriting. The tools required are quite simple: a piece of paper and a pen, or—if you prefer—your smartphone or computer.

The idea behind this exercise is that we carry a lot of thoughts and feelings inside of us, and we often do not feel that there is anyone with whom we can share those thoughts and feelings. By freewriting whatever is on your mind or in your heart, you can give yourself the space to say whatever you need to say without judgment. It can be quite helpful in clearing out overly saturated thoughts and feelings, and often can support clarity in working through obstacles you are facing. The following are some prompts and suggestions you might consider writing about:

- I'm feeling scared for my teen because . . .

- How can I better support my teen?

- What are my dreams for my teen's future?

- How can I get involved in the LGBTQ+ community?

- What kind of relationship do I want to have with my teen?

- Ways I can take care of myself:

- Ways I can show my love for my teen:

- I feel so angry because . . .

- I feel so lost because . . .

- What makes me feel hopeful?

The Teenage Years Are Hard Enough—Don't Make Them Harder

If it's your goal to support and help your LGBTQ+ teen, then I encourage you to spend some time focusing on how you can adjust your parenting to be less stress-inducing for your child. Under even the best of conditions, the teenage years are hard to maneuver. Extensive research has shown that when teens feel that they can be themselves at home, and that their families accept and nurture them, they will feel much more confident in dealing with the relentless torment and hostility in other environments. Talk to your teen and figure out how you can make their lives just a little bit easier so that they can focus on learning, building their self-confidence, and developing the inner resilience to be whoever they are meant to be. Do not allow them to go to bed wondering if they matter to you or if you still love them. You have the power to give your teen the strength to persevere, with you standing by them every step of the way.

How You Parent Is the Primary Shaper of Your LGBTQ+ Teen's Experience

How a parent responds to their LGBTQ+ teen is a critical influence on how that teen will react, cope, and manage their personal development, through their coming-out experience and beyond. Parents who respond with a lack of compassion; who show no effort to understand; and who lack patience, acceptance, and accessibility will negatively impact their teen's coming-out experience. On the other hand, teens who feel they can trust the unconditional love of their primary caregivers often have a more optimistic view of how they will be received by society at large, which gives them the confidence and courage it takes to express their full selves. Teens need to know they are accepted—at the very least tolerated—by the biggest and most significant figures in their life.

LGBTQ+ teens are very sensitive to any level of judgment and criticism from their parents. If they feel rejected, they often will shut down and isolate, or they may lash out. Sadly, many fear for their emotional, social, and physical safety for being different. I encourage parents to consider how you are currently engaging with your teen and ask yourself what message you are communicating about how you feel and think about them being LGBTQ+.

Let Them Be Who They Are

Allowing your LGBTQ+ teen to express themself can be challenging, especially if you don't feel as though you fully understand their identity and choices; however, it is essential for the overall positive and healthy development of your teen. For the first time in their life, they are learning how to think for themself and decide who they want to become. Teens are seeking acceptance and approval, and to feel normal, despite their feelings of insecurity and doubt. Teens are contemplating many new ideas, experiences, looks, friendships, and the abundance of ways they can express themselves. It's through these adolescent trials and tribulations that they can ultimately figure out what they like and what is important to them, and gain clarity and strength in their voice and identity.

Do you really need to make that comment on their outfit or hair color choice? Your teen already deals with judgment and criticism from their peers. You have the opportunity to provide them with a home that is safe and free from any judgment or ridicule. By offering your teen love and unconditional acceptance, you can help them learn to love themself.

Above All, Be Their Biggest Cheerleader

As a parent, your LGBTQ+ teen is looking to you to be their biggest supporter. Even though they might act at times as though they do not care for your opinion and it does not matter what you think, this could not be farther from the truth. You are the single most important influencer in your teen's life, and every teenager I have had the pleasure of working with has always wanted to feel support from their parent.

Your teenager is afraid of messing up, making the wrong decision, and disappointing you. They are hungry for approval and support, and if they do not receive it from you, then they will go elsewhere and seek it from others. Teens will turn to others who will give them the reassurance and confidence to be themselves, but might be at risk because some people may not have their best interests at heart. Though this might not be easy to do if you are still coming to terms with your teen's LGBTQ+ identity, it is critical that your teenager knows they have your unconditional support.

Connection Tips

Listen, truly listen – Your teen is communicating with you often, not only through their words, but also through their actions and body language. They are telling you when they need attention, when they are scared, when they are worried, and if they want to talk. If your teen feels that you value their feelings, thoughts, and struggles, they will be more likely to turn to you.

Be curious and step out of your comfort zone – Many parents are trying to work through their own process. Go and seek out your own answers through support groups like PFLAG and other LGBTQ+ community resources and platforms. Then share with your teen what you have learned. This is a great way for parents to show their teens they are open and putting in the effort.

Stand up for your teen – Just like your teen, you may also experience judgment and rejection from others because of their LGBTQ+ identity. It's important for your teen to see you defending and protecting them from further harm from others. If you are religious and your church has expressed hateful rhetoric, then you might need to find a new congregation. If some of your friends and family make anti-LGBTQ+ comments, then let them know that is not okay and you will no longer tolerate their comments.

Be accessible – Recognize that your teen may not feel like talking at the exact moment you do. You can invite them into a conversation and still respect their decision not to engage. Let them know you are available when they are ready.

Conclusion

I hope this chapter provided you with more clarity and understanding of your role as a protector and guardian of your LGBTQ+ teen. I know the amount of terminology can be quite intimidating, but the most important thing is your willingness to learn and be open. Remember, it's your relationship with your LGBTQ+ teen that is a fundamental indicator of how your teen will adjust to their gender identity and sexual orientation. I have laid out some of the different challenges your teen could be dealing with, and I hope this supports you in having a better sense of how to be there for them. As we move forward to the next chapter, I will provide you with even more tools and parenting support.

■ ■ ■ ■ ■ ■ ■ ■ ■ ■

"We must be willing to let go of the life we have planned, so as to have the life that is waiting for us."

—Joseph Campbell

PART II

The Path Forward

In part 2 of this book, we begin to explore how to create a strong foundation for your LGBTQ+ teen, so you can then feel more confident initiating difficult and sensitive conversations. We will then focus on how to nurture your connection with your teen and empower them to embrace their authentic self. Finally, it is critical to recognize the value of surrounding your teen with a supportive community; you do not have to do this alone. By the end of part 2, I hope you will feel more empowered in your parental role and experience more togetherness with your teen.

"Nothing in life is to be feared, it is only to be understood. Now is the time to understand more, so that we can fear less."

—*Marie Curie*

CHAPTER THREE

Build a Strong Foundation for Your LGBTQ+ Teen

In order to build a strong foundation for your LGBTQ+ teen, you need to first get in touch with yourself and establish some basic guidelines for how you are going to parent. This chapter is intended to guide you through some self-reflections and help you understand yourself better, in order to positively influence your teen's foundation. Try to recall what your own teen years were like. Your experiences shape who you are, how you parent, and the expectations you have of yourself and your teen. What might be some of your own childhood or adult wounds that are feeding into your thoughts, feelings, and reactions to your teen's coming out? In a year, five years, or twenty years from now, how would you like your adult child to characterize and describe how you were as a parent? The answers to these thought-provoking questions will help you shape and model character-building values that you want your teen to build on, such as compassion, self-respect, respect for others, and confidence.

Alexander and Jordan

Alexander is a single father of four and his 17-year-old son, Jordan, came out as gay almost a year ago now. Alexander grew up in a rough neighborhood in South Central Los Angeles. As a child, he attended church almost every Sunday and found refuge in his religion, which helped him manage his own struggles. Alexander continues to be active in his church and socializes with the congregation. However, he has struggled since Jordan came out to him, unsure about how he, his friends, his family, and his congregation will accept Jordan being a gay man.

Alexander and Jordan talk often about Alexander's own childhood, hearing slurs directed towards his peers such as *faggot*, *fairy*, *sissy*, and *princess*. He remembers classmates who were suspected of being gay, or considered simply not straight-acting enough, being teased and bullied relentlessly in the locker room and the hallways. Jordan reassures his father he is okay, but Alexander still worries this will also be Jordan's experience. Alexander and Jordan talk about where they live and if Jordan fears he might fall victim of further discrimination for being gay and Black. Alexander feels some relief that Jordan can pass for a straight athlete, as he himself was shocked when Jordan came out to him because he just did not fit the effeminate gay man stereotype. Alexander knows that if he wants a stronger relationship with Jordan, then he will have to connect with him, so Alexander reached out to a local Black LGBTQ+ resource center and he attends PFLAG (Parents, Families, and Friends of Lesbians and Gays) meetings. Alexander and Jordan continue to grow their relationship.

Growing Up Is Hard for Everyone

Adolescence is one of the most significant developmental and transitional periods of one's life, and for many reasons, it is an especially trying time for many LGBTQ+ teens. There are so many pressures they place on themselves, many of which they are not completely prepared to handle mentally or developmentally. It's a period when teens want to fit in, but at the same time also want to find and be their true selves. LGBTQ+ teens often report feeling unhappy about how they look and constantly comparing themselves to others. Transgender teens in particular struggle with the disconnect between who they see in the mirror and their true gender identity; they also face an exceptionally higher degree of bullying and threats compared to other identities within the LGBTQ+ spectrum.

During adolescence, peer inclusion is particularly important, and teens spend immense mental energy focusing on being accepted and feeling safe. Many teens also yearn to be part of the "cool" group, perhaps learning for the first time there is a social hierarchy. LGBTQ+ teens often have the added stress of fearing rejection if their sexual orientation and gender identity were made public. Depending on where you live, there may also be additional cultural pressures due to an additional lack of inclusion for LGBTQ+ teens of color.

No Matter How Old Your Child Gets, They Will Always Look to You

Just because your teen has come out as LGBTQ+ doesn't change that you are still their parent, and they still need you. Your teen continues to watch your every move, wondering what you might be thinking about them. You are still their biggest influencer and biggest role model. They want your approval and to know that you will stand by them, even when they make decisions you do not like or agree with. They need to know that you have their back and that you will help them through this adjustment period. Reaffirming your love for your teen may be hard to do when you don't agree with or understand their decisions, but it is incredibly important to let them know your love is unconditional.

SELF-ASSESSMENT: WHAT ARE YOUR EXPECTATIONS FOR YOURSELF AS A PARENT?

Our expectations influence how we live our lives and how we experience the world around us. As a parent, it is helpful to be aware and know what your expectations are for yourself. Many parents think their expectations of their children will—and should—always produce outcomes aligned with those expectations, but as you have probably discovered, that couldn't be farther from the truth. You might have heard that "expectations are premeditated resentments." Indeed, parents often make the mistake of connecting their level of happiness with the degree to which their expectations are fulfilled.

In this exercise, examine your own expectations so you can become more aware and consider whether they still work for you.

1. Grab a blank piece of paper and a pen.

2. Draw a table with three labeled columns: what my teen can expect from me, what my teen cannot expect from me, and what I expect from my teen.

3. Find a quiet space where you can think about each section and write down your thoughts.

4. After you are done with each section, you can use this chart to self-reflect and consider what changes you can make that will help improve your relationship with your teen.

5. Consider the following table and explore whether any of these entries resonate with your parenting values and expectations.

WHAT MY TEEN CAN EXPECT FROM ME
• I will listen • I won't judge • I will love them always • I will support them • I will encourage them • I won't smother them

WHAT MY TEEN CANNOT EXPECT FROM ME
• Allowing them to hurt themself • Letting go of academic expectations • Letting them go out without telling me where they are going

WHAT I EXPECT FROM MY TEEN
• Talk to me even when it's hard • Make safe decisions • Love themself • Respect house rules • Let me know when help is needed

Start with Empathy

What exactly does it mean to be empathetic? Empathy is more than just caring for your LGBTQ+ teen. It is about being able to see yourself in their shoes. By being empathetic, you are attempting to see their world through their eyes, ears, heart, and mind. It can be hard to let go of your ideas and opinions of what is best for your teen, but it is important to try to be open to supporting your teen's perspective on what they want and need. Based on my professional experience working with many LGBTQ+ teens and their parents, I'm confident your teen simply wants to feel accepted and validated for being themself.

You can get better at being empathetic by incorporating a few simple things:

Ask questions without judgment. Engage with genuine curiosity to learn about your teenager's perspective on what it is like being LGBTQ+ and what they want. Refraining from immediately voicing your opinion will help open up communication in your relationship.

Set aside your assumptions and preconceived beliefs. Honor your teen's individuality, and you will find you still have shared values and beliefs. They are still the same person you have always loved. Be humble and open to learning new things about them and about yourself.

Join an LGBTQ+ support group such as PFLAG or online groups. This will help you build compassion as you hear the experiences of others. You will learn from the stories of how other parents are being empathetic to their teens.

REMEMBER, YOU WERE A TEEN ONCE

It can be easy for all of us to forget we were once teenagers. Even though you might have never questioned your gender identity or your sexual orientation, it can be helpful for you to think back to what your adolescence was like. Can you remember peers being mistreated for being different? Try to think about what challenges you faced in school, your family, and the community you grew up in. In what ways were your own interests and values judged and devalued? Think of what got you in trouble at home, and how you and your parents dealt with those differences. What was it like for you to finally find and be yourself? The more you can remember what it was like for you as a teen, the more understanding you will be as a parent.

Acknowledge Your Teenager's Experience Is Different from Yours

I cannot emphasize enough the importance of validating and seeing your LGBTQ+ teen for who they are through the lens of the world they are living in now. Although there are some basic similar experiences (peer pressure, academic pressures, romantic infatuations) that are shared across different generations of teenagers, there are new pressures you did not have to contend with (cyberbullying, media overconsumption, faster-paced family life). Today's teens are living in a world that is moving rapidly, and they are just trying to stay above water between multiple classes, volunteer responsibilities, part-time jobs, sports, clubs, and social media, all while also trying to appease their peers by being fun and likeable and having the right fashion. On top of all this, the current generation is constantly bombarded with images of how imperfect they are.

Ultimately, they want to know you truly understand that their experiences are different from yours. Take the time to talk to your teen and hear from them what it is like to be a teenager these days. When your teen's friends are hanging out at your home, what are they giggling and talking about? You will learn a lot about teen life, but most importantly, you will start to better understand *your* teen's life.

It is quite common for parents to share with their teens what their experiences growing up were like and how they were raised. This can sometimes feel like an unfair comparison for the teen, further emphasizing that their parent simply does not understand. In the following example, Doug (parent) and Jessie (a 15-year-old transgender girl) are having an interaction at their home. I offer this exchange as an example of how you can take the opportunity to share in a more constructive way.

Doug: Jessie, I'm doing laundry. Do you have anything for me that needs washing?

Jessie: That stack over there.

Doug: You mean these? Aren't these your sister's clothes?

Jessie: No, Dad, they're mine (sigh).

Doug: I'm still getting used to this new way of dressing. When I was your age, there would be no way I could get away with wearing girl's clothes. My friends at school would think I was a freak.

Jessie: Things are different now, and most kids don't care so much what I wear. Some do, but I feel more confident in girl's clothes.

Doug: Jessie, I'm sorry. I don't mean to be insensitive. I get it, times are different now and you want to be able to make your own choices and express yourself how you want. I want for you to be yourself and I love you no matter what you are wearing.

Jessie: I know, Dad. I know it's still hard.

Doug: It sure is, but we are going to work through this. And I will stop making hurtful comparisons and comments. I love you.

In this exchange, Doug was communicating how he is adjusting. He displayed empathy by identifying and honoring his daughter's need to make her own choices and express who she is. Doug also owns his insensitive misstep and reassures Jessie she can dress how she wants and always has his continuing love.

Deal with Your Own Feelings First

I know you must be going through a whole lot of your own emotions right now. As a society, we have been told that positive emotions such as joy, elation, or excitement are good and should be embraced. On the other hand, we learn that negative emotions such as hopelessness, sadness, and pessimism should be silenced or suppressed. We are not taught how to handle feelings such as disappointment or fear very well. The reality is that the full range of emotions has value and contains normal responses to the different situations and challenges we face. All emotions are useful and informative, and understanding why we feel the way we do can help facilitate thoughtful and deliberate changes to better ourselves and our relationships with those we love.

Chances are you have overheard negative comments about LGBTQ+ individuals from your own family members and your community. You have heard far too often news of prejudice and discrimination against LGBTQ+ people. This may cause you to feel fear and uncertainty for your teen and their future. I am encouraging you, as scary as it might be, to sit with your feelings for a bit and spend some time understanding what your feelings mean to you. You can start by naming them and exploring where they come from: fear, shame, anxiety, scars from childhood, religious programming, unfulfilled expectations, and so on. Think about what you want to do with those feelings and how you can choose to respond to them. How can you move through your emotions so that you can figure out how to be the parent you want to be? This is about taking care of yourself, so you can also take care of your teen.

Build Your Self-Esteem as a Parent

Parenting is a difficult job. Coming to terms with your teen being on the LGBTQ+ spectrum can be triggering for you on many different levels, and it might breed insecurity and vulnerability. *This is normal,* and countless other parents around the world are also trying to figure it out.

It is hard to own your shortcomings and sensitivities. No parent wants to feel inadequate or vulnerable. Recognize that you have already done a wonderful job of raising and instilling values in your teen. Also know that their sexual orientation and gender identity has nothing to do with you—you did not make them LGBTQ+; it is who *they* are. If they have already come out to you, take some credit for teaching them how to be courageous and instilling strength of character, as evidenced by their ability to be honest with themself about who they really are. You have already come a long way in teaching your teen how to be great in their own special ways. Stop comparing yourself to other parents and look at what obstacles you have already overcome in your own life and parenthood journey.

Be a Leader They Can Count On

When was the last time you considered what type of parent you want to be to your LGBTQ+ teen? Have you ever considered your teen has been looking to you their entire life, and you have been showing them how they are supposed to be? Your parenting ideas, values, beliefs, and style determine how effective you are as a leader of your family. For you to be a positive person of influence, you first need to be aware of how you have been engaging and interacting in the world around you and what kind of behavior you are modeling to your child. Practicing self-awareness can help you lead your teen toward a positive, healthy adjustment and acceptance of their LGBTQ+ self.

Your LGBTQ+ teen is looking to you for guidance and direction on how to maneuver through their journey of self-discovery and self-confidence. One of the most helpful skills a parent can teach their teen is how to take a thoughtful pause to think about how to best overcome and strategize effectively, instead of mindlessly reacting to emotions and unfamiliar situations. Help your teen recognize and harness their strengths and talents toward creating their best self. How are you fostering their independent thinking, success, values, and learning?

Tips for Better Conversations

Timing is everything – Picking the right time can make a world of difference. Is your teen hungry, tired, stressed out studying for an exam, or rushing to school? Time your conversations for when you are both likely to be at your best.

Location, location, location – I generally suggest finding a spot that is neutral, calm, and private, and where you are both comfortable. Simply asking your teen where they would like to have the conversation can do the trick (and helps them feel that their opinion and preference are respected).

Be aware of body language – Face each other, maintain comfortable eye contact, avoid crossing your arms, and sit at a comfortable proximity. Be aware of mannerisms or touch that could be misconstrued.

Emotional awareness – Help each other be more aware of emotional reactions during the conversation. If either of you is getting angry or no longer listening, then that is your cue to take a time-out.

Practice deep listening – Really listen to what your teen is saying, without getting defensive or immediately reacting. You don't need to have an opinion about everything. Reflect back to them what you heard and ask for clarification on things you didn't understand.

Model Important Values for Your Teen

Values are those pillars that provide structure in knowing right from wrong, and which also guide us through all aspects and decisions we make about how we live. Keep in mind that your teen has been learning values from you their entire life based on how you respond to challenging situations, how you treat other people, how you show caring for others, how you deal with difficult people, and how you respect yourself.

Your teen, for the rest of their life, will be making critical decisions based on the very values you planted in them. Hopefully, those values are solid, and they contribute to a positive sense of self. When an LGBTQ+ teen is clear and solid in their convictions, they will then be more motivated to make empowering, strengthening, and validating decisions to nurture their spirit and allow themself to flourish. They will be more likely to make smart decisions when confronted with solicitations of drugs and alcohol, have the confidence to be their authentic self, be in healthy relationships, and recognize when a friend or romantic interest is toxic.

SHOW RESPECT FOR OTHERS

Parents who model respect toward others teach teens how to respect the people in their lives—most importantly, themselves. They learn from you how to treat others who are different from them, or who have a different opinion. They gain the trust to share themself with you when they see that you respect others and treat them with dignity.

HAVE CONFIDENCE IN WHO YOU ARE

There are going to be times when, as a parent, you feel like you are doing it all wrong, or like you lack direction on how to manage a situation. It is absolutely normal to feel this way. I encourage parents during these times to remember their successes, and although it might not feel like it at this moment, you do have many successes from which you can draw confidence and hope. As unfamiliar and overwhelming as this experience may be for you, honor yourself for still showing up for your LGBTQ+ teen. It takes inner strength to move through this uncertain journey.

DEMONSTRATE RESILIENCE IN THE FACE OF ADVERSITY

LGBTQ+ teenagers can be highly sensitive toward different types of adversity, and you can model for your child how to best manage difficult situations. Teach your teen how to recognize challenges and show them they do not have to allow their emotions to overwhelm and bulldoze them. Model for them what it looks like to get back up and try again after disappointments and failures. Support them in those moments when they feel as though they have failed, and encourage them to get back up with fortitude and self-compassion.

Have Compassion for Yourself

Compassion—for both yourself and your LGBTQ+ teen—is critical during this journey. Give yourself the gift of self-care and kindness during your experiences of suffering, perceptions of failure, and imperfections. Consider how you can add some of the following tips to your life:

Acceptance – Accept your current situation at face value, and accept that at this moment you are doing the best you can.

Change your story – We all have those negative and critical voices in our head. But are they telling the truth? Try embracing a more self-loving affirmation, such as "I am enough."

Name it – Some examples of this are "This is painful" or "This is overwhelming." Often, when we name our difficult feelings, they lose some of their power over us.

Remember to think about what you need in the moment, be kind to yourself, and stop beating yourself up.

Managing a Modern Family Can Be Tricky

There may be extenuating circumstances that are making your adjustment and journey as a parent even more difficult. I am speaking about modern family factors such as cultural differences between partners, socioeconomic challenges, divorce, blended families, single parenting, and adoption. It's important to recognize and honor the distinct and individualized qualities of your family, as no two families are exactly the same. Your specific circumstances will affect how you approach and work through these challenges and support your LGBTQ+ teen.

No one solution is perfect for every family, so think about what you need to focus on to work through your particular challenges. For instance, a family who has multiple generations living under the same roof will be dealing with different challenges than a single parent or adoptive parents. Regardless of the unique challenges you are facing, there are solutions, and you don't have to deal with them on your own. But it's up to you to seek out the resources and supports available to you.

SET THE TONE FOR YOUR OTHER CHILDREN

If you have multiple children, you are setting the tone for how to adjust to having an LGBTQ+ teen as a family member. Your other children are going to have their own reactions, but it is up to you to model the compassion and acceptance you want them to show their sibling. Be clear on your expectations and how, as a family, you will continue to treat each other with respect. You can ask your LGBTQ+ teen how they would like for you to set the tone with your other children. It is also important to consider what is developmentally appropriate for each child and to explain things in way they will understand.

GET ON THE SAME PAGE AS A CO-PARENT

You probably won't get on the same page overnight, especially if you are already dealing with preexisting issues with your co-parent. My suggestion is to hear one another out. Talk about your concerns and accept that you are not going to agree on everything. Start with the things you do agree on. Focus on the bigger goals you have as co-parents. Showing your LGBTQ+ teen that you can be on different pages, but still be concerned and care for their overall success and growth, is key.

WHAT TO DO WHEN YOUR PARTNER DOESN'T AGREE WITH YOUR APPROACH

Most people think the only acceptable answer is to be in agreement. But I have found over the years that what most people want is to be heard and understood. We want to be validated and we want to feel that we know what we are doing. So if you and your partner or co-parent are not in sync with how to approach and deal with coming to terms with your LGBTQ+ teen, then listen, reflect, and keep the lines of communication open. Focus on your goals, which are to support your child and to support one another through this. If you continue to have difficulties, it may be helpful to seek out counseling together.

20 QUESTIONS

One of the ways I encourage teens and their parents to build a connection is through an exercise called 20 Questions. This exercise can be a great way learn more about one another.

1. Take a few pieces of paper and cut them up into even, two-inch, square pieces.

2. Distribute the blank pieces between the participants. If both parents play or if there are more family members who want to play, then you can modify the exercise by adding more blank pieces of paper to even it out.

3. Each person then writes a question they would like to ask the other participants on their blank pieces of paper. The questions can be as deep or light as the participants choose. The idea is to ask questions that will help you understand and know each other better. For example, "Who is your favorite LGBTQ+ celebrity and why?" or "What is your biggest fear?"

4. Each piece of paper is folded so you cannot read the questions, and they are then put into a bowl or any container that can be easily drawn from.

5. Each person goes around and picks a question out of the bowl and answers, until all the questions have been answered.

Whatever You Do, Be Consistent

Your LGBTQ+ teen may have struggled for a very long time with worry about how their orientation will be received. They continue to be riddled with anxiety that you will no longer love them and that they will be treated differently. The best thing you can do is to treat them the same as you did before they came out to you. Keep a consistent and familiar structure to your day and how you run your household. Try to avoid any huge changes. I understand things might not be exactly the same, but keeping consistency in your expectations of your child and how you show up for them is important.

Your LGBTQ+ teen is looking for a sense of safety and security. Your role is to provide a familiar, loving, and safe home environment. Your teen in going through a tumultuous period trying to figure out what their new normal is. Providing a home base where they are clear on what is expected of them and confident that you will be there to support and guide them through it all will help make it a bit easier for your teen.

Take It One Step at a Time

If you hear nothing else from me, I want you to hear this: *You cannot rush the process!* Unfortunately, what you are dealing with and what your teenager is going through are going to take time, but as long as you remain open and keep turning toward one another, you will be all right. It is normal to feel lost, confused, conflicted, insufficient, and unsure at times, but you do not need to let these emotions control you.

The hard part is truly trying to make sense of your feelings and to understand why you feel the way you do. My guess is that you have your own wounds you have been trying to work through. You are trying to figure out what having an LGBTQ+ teen means for you and what it says about you, and what it all means for a new future. There will be moments when you feel that you have a good grasp on things, and then other times when you are just trying to make it through the day. This is normal. Just keep getting back up and taking one more step forward.

Conclusion

I hope you found this chapter encouraging and a reminder that you already have many strengths you can build upon as a parent. You have already been building a strong foundation with your teen; now you just need to do some fine-tuning. It can be incredibly helpful if you can take steps outside of your comfort zone and identify the areas where you feel vulnerable or where you can grow. No parent is going to handle every situation and challenge in the ideal and perfect way, but every setback is an opportunity to learn and grow. Keep going and focus on your parental goals and values. Focus on showing compassion for your teen and teaching them resilience.

Now that you have more clarity and self-awareness—and hopefully a bit more confidence—let's transition to how to have the much-needed and overdue conversations with your LGBTQ+ teen. It's time for you to be brave as you begin to delve into your teen's world a bit more.

"We are not what other people say we are. We are who we know ourselves to be, and we are what we love."

—*Laverne Cox*

CHAPTER FOUR

Initiate Difficult Conversations

I would expect you have some questions and curiosities you would like to talk about with your LGBTQ+ teen, however, the mere thought of having the conversation can be intimidating and overwhelming. This chapter is intended to offer you some support and tools to help you feel more confident in initiating difficult conversations with your teen.

Mark and Steven

Mark and his 16-year-old adopted son, Steven, haven't been very successful with prior attempts to talk. Mark has felt for a very long time that he and his son avoid one-on-one time together. One day, Mark decides to go to Steven's room and asks if they can talk. Mark shares that he has always felt envious of Steven's closeness with his mother and would like to build a closer relationship with him. Mark further expresses his sadness that he never had a close relationship with his own father and that he would be interested in hearing more about Steven's life and being more of a supportive father figure to him. Steven just sits there and listens and doesn't say much at all. With that reaction, Mark can't fathom addressing his suspicion of Steven's sexual orientation, so Mark tells Steven he doesn't have to respond at that moment, but asks Steven to think about what he has shared. Mark thanks his son for hearing him out and again asserts that Steven can come to him whenever he is ready to talk more about it.

Conversations That Seem Scary to You Are Much Scarier for Your Teen

I know the idea of talking with your teen could be frightening to you, but the truth is your LGBTQ+ teen is probably even more frightened than you are. From your teen's vantage point, they feel they have a lot more to lose should you not accept their sexual orientation, gender identity, or any other aspect of who they are. They depend so much on you for their basic sense of safety and security. By opening up, your teen risks possible rejection, lack of acceptance of who they are, losing your love for them, potentially being put out onto the streets and being homeless, having no means to financially support themself, and the loss of everyone and everything they hold near and dear.

It is also quite common for children to take on the responsibility for the imperfections in their home life. Coming to you as an LGBTQ+ teen brings all types of worries for them, and they do not want to add to the troubles they see you already dealing with. They may be afraid they will get in trouble or you won't understand them. They may fear that their coming out will ruin their family, or that their fear of being a disappointment will be confirmed. Have compassion for the vulnerability both you and your child may be feeling.

Be Proactive

A lot of people tend to try to avoid problems, or they hope the problem will just miraculously go away. But the reality is there isn't anyone who is going to come along and fix the problem for you. My advice is for you is to do your best at being proactive and dealing with difficulties head-on. Ask yourself: What can I do to feel more empowered and in control?

As a parent, it's your job to be a role model and to point out concerns that your LGBTQ+ teen might not see. Being proactive shows your teenager they, too, can approach their own challenges in a way that helps them learn lifelong skills they can benefit from. A proactive approach encourages teens to keep trying to improve their situation. It will help you and help them feel a little less lonely, a little less anxious, and a little less powerless. Many of the situations we have encountered in our lives are resolved with ongoing proactive efforts that support us and build our confidence. You can make difficult situations better.

Problems Aren't Going to Solve Themselves

Since your LGBTQ+ teen has come out to you, or since you started to suspect there is something different about your child, it may be that a lot still feels unresolved. The only way to resolve these issues is by being brave and walking through the fire to face them head on.

You are going to have to deal with the challenges your LGBTQ+ teen has brought to the surface. It may not be easy, but in the long run you will have much better results than if you choose to do nothing. If how you have been trying to manage the challenges is not getting you the results you want, then ask yourself what you can do differently. Remember, you also do not have to deal with them on your own. I encourage you to reach out to a close, trusted friend, an understanding pastor, professional help, or support groups and organizations for parents of LGBTQ+ kids. Stop being so hard on yourself and thinking you should have everything figured out. Your baby steps are just as valuable as the sprints.

Maybe you have been holding off on that important conversation, afraid to ask the big question that's been on your mind. What are you waiting for? Many people get stuck or paralyzed from taking any action, and they end up making their worries and challenges even bigger; the silence and distance between them and their teen grows until it feels even more insurmountable. Stop worrying about saying or doing everything perfectly with your LGBTQ+ teen. Accept that you might say or do the wrong thing, and if you do, take a pause, apologize, restart, and try again.

How to Talk to Your Teen So They Listen

Lead by example – Teens will behave in ways modeled for them. If you show them you can hear them out, no matter what you might think or feel, they will be more likely to do the same for you.

Stop talking so much! – Parents can sometimes talk way too much and be too vocal about their opinions. This can cause your teen to feel overly stimulated, overwhelmed, and silenced. Stick to the important points and keep it simple. There's nothing like a lecture to make a teen tune out.

Watch the volume – If you find yourself raising your voice, you will be less likely to keep your child's attention and more likely to get a defensive reaction.

Keep calm – These conversations are hard enough, and when you start to get overly emotional, angry, or anxious, your teen might begin to feel unsafe and tune you out. You can always take a break and return to the conversation when you feel calmer.

Adopt a Policy of Open Communication

If it is your goal to have more open communication with your LGBTQ+ teen, then it will be important to first spend some time thinking about what might be keeping you from achieving this goal. Many parents tell me in the therapy room they want their teen to be more responsive and available, but when we delve into talking about how *they* have been engaging, it's no wonder their LGBTQ+ teen does not speak with them.

Even though you say you want to have more open communication with your LGBTQ+ teen, you might be giving off signals of judgment or disapproval. Teens want to feel safe and don't want to be further judged for the things they are curious about or situations they are dealing with. Being able to regulate your own emotional reactions and judgments will support your teen coming to you more. Asking your child what support would be helpful to them will also demonstrate efforts to better listen and understand. It might be that your teen simply needs a safe place to vent and does not want you to offer solutions or advice, but to simply validate what they are going through. It can be helpful to ask them directly what kind of feedback they want before giving it.

BE OPEN TO CONVERSATIONS EVEN WHEN IT'S NOT CONVENIENT FOR YOU

It's important to understand your LGBTQ+ teen has likely been feeling very alone for quite a long time, and is already feeling insecure about reaching out. The perception of your accessibility is very important to consider if you want your communication with your teen to improve. If they want to talk, take time to stop what you are doing and give them your full attention.

WHEN YOUR TEEN JUST WON'T LISTEN: WRITE A LETTER

Parents often report they simply cannot get their LGBTQ+ teen to listen and they have no idea what to do. Sometimes the idea of sitting down with your teen and talking about difficult matters is just too hard, or you have already had one too many unsuccessful attempts. If talking directly feels impossible, try expressing yourself in a letter. Not only does this provide you an outlet, but you also have an opportunity to read it over and revise so it says exactly what you want to say. You can make sure you are communicating in a way your teen will be able to hear you, and you can also avoid any hurtful or offensive communication. If you want, you can have your partner or another trusted confidant read it first and give you feedback. Then, when you have the completed version, you can present it to your teen and let them know you'd like to talk about it when they are ready. You can even invite them to write you a letter, too.

Struggles Your LGBTQ+ Teen May Be Facing

Being a teenager in the modern age is hard enough, but LGBTQ+ teens often feel the burden much more acutely than their peers. Without the right support and attention, there are many issues that have the potential to cause long-term pain and difficulties for your child. LGBTQ+ teens are more likely to suffer from mental health issues, low self-esteem, substance-abuse issues, and eating disorders due to the internalization of chronic and extreme stress from bullying, violence, social pressures, isolation, and discrimination. Many turn to risky and self-destructive behaviors to try to silence and numb the emotional pain and mental misery they experience by simply being different. The good news is with your compassion and fierce support, your child will be able to navigate these difficulties with grace, confidence, strong values, and a secure sense of self.

ANXIETY, DEPRESSION, AND MENTAL HEALTH

LGBTQ+ teens report a dishearteningly higher frequency and degree of anxiety, depression, and other mental health challenges compared to their heterosexual and cisgender peers. In some research, the disparity is two times greater for LGBTQ+ teens. Chronic social, emotional, relational, and familial fears, along with a high degree of bullying and lack of acceptance, are a few of the factors contributing to the alarming rates of mental illness. These stressors are amplified even more for LGBTQ+ teens of color.

CONFUSION

It is not uncommon for LGBTQ+ teens to report confusion around their sexual orientation, gender identity, and how to best cope. This confusion is compounded by their internal conflict between who they are and what society expects of them. Social and cultural stigmas attached to ideas about homosexuality, misconceptions about what it means to be LGBTQ+, and limited positive role models can make it more difficult to figure things out. Teens can feel ill-equipped to handle their attractions and identities that don't fit neatly into mainstream definitions of "normal," as well as the new emotions they are experiencing for the first time.

FEAR

One of the biggest fears a lot of LGBTQ+ teens face is being discovered by their peers, and even more so by their families. More than likely, your teen has already heard and seen how other LGBTQ+ teens get mistreated. About 50 percent of gay boys and about 20 percent of lesbians have been verbally or physically harmed at school. Fear of harassment does not only occur at school, but for many, harassment also occurs at home, too. Fear of rejection and homelessness are also commonly reported among LGBTQ+ teens.

BULLYING

For LGBTQ+ teens, bullying is as much as double the threat compared to their heterosexual and cisgender peers. We now have various digital and social media platforms (group texts, Facebook, Snapchat, Instagram) where cruelty and hate is public and seemingly inescapable, on the screen, for your LGBTQ+ teen to be tormented by over and over again. Bullying is a serious matter and has been noted by researchers as a common cause of self-harm and suicide. I cannot encourage you enough to educate yourself about the signs of bullying so you can provide refuge and support for your teen. They do not have to deal with this kind of fear alone.

ROLE PLAY

Role-playing is a helpful way to ease your anxiety and help you feel more prepared to talk with your teen about important topics (such as self-harm, safer sex, and relationships). This is also a way to minimize the chances your strong emotions will come out through hurtful words or reactions, which cannot be retracted. By doing this exercise, you can help increase the chances of having a more successful conversation with your teen that both of you can feel good about.

1. Find someone who knows you and your teen well.

2. Think about the things you want to say to your teen and how you would like the conversation to go.

3. You play you, and your support person plays your teen.

4. Try out a few practice-run conversations with your support person.

5. In between runs, talk with your support person about what you did well and what you could do better.

6. Run through it as many times as you need to until you feel ready to have the actual conversation with your teen.

7. The goal is not to be 100 percent anxiety-free. The goal is to significantly reduce your anxiety so you can express yourself clearly and thoughtfully.

FEELING UNSAFE

Where your teen falls on the LGBTQ+ spectrum, their ability to pass as heterosexual and cisgender, and your community's attitudes can greatly influence your teen's sense of safety. Transgender teens report an even higher degree of concern for their safety compared to other identities. For instance, transgender individuals still do not have access to safe bathroom accommodations in many schools and other public places. In dating situations, a transgender teen may not know how to share their true identity with a potential date, fearing it could lead to a dangerous situation. Emotional, sexual, relational, academic, political, and home safety are also concerns for LGBTQ+ teens.

SUBSTANCE ABUSE

The prevalence of substance abuse and addiction in LGBTQ+ individuals is two to three times the rate of the population as a whole. The emotional and mental anguish of social isolation, prejudice, bullying, low self-worth, and family problems are often too much to deal with, and teens will self-medicate to escape or numb their pain. For the LGBTQ+ teens who are ethnic and racial minorities, the rates are even higher. The good news is that LGBTQ+ teens with emotional support and safety at home and within the community are less likely to turn to drug and alcohol use and abuse.

EATING DISORDERS

A struggle for LGBTQ+ teens often not spoken about is eating disorders. A study compared heterosexual and LGBTQ+ youth and found a higher percentage of LGBTQ+ youth reporting binge eating and purging, some starting as early as 12 to 14 years old. A 2013 study found disordered weight-control behaviors (such as restricting, purging, and using diet pills) in one in five gay and bisexual high school boys. By far, the highest rates of eating disorders and behaviors like diet pill and/or laxative use are reported in transgender teens.

SELF-HARMING

Self-harming behaviors, also known as NSSI (non-suicidal self-injury), are another struggle LGBTQ+ teens face, which are also correlated to suicidal ideation and risk. There are different ways teens self-harm, such as cutting, burning, scratching, hitting and punching themselves, piercing, picking at existing wounds, and pulling one's hair out. These forms of behaviors can reflect the immense shame LGBTQ+ teens feel. If your teen exhibits any of these behaviors, seek professional help so they can learn healthier ways of dealing with their painful emotional and situational struggles. Again, a strong support network will help minimize the risk of them developing self-harming behaviors.

SUICIDE

Suicide and suicidal ideation are serious concerns and should never be taken lightly or ignored. According to research by the Centers for Disease Control, for those within gender and sexual minorities, rates of suicidal contemplation are three times greater, and for suicide attempts, they are almost five times greater. Suicide attempts by LGBTQ+ teens often require medical attention due to poisoning, overdose, or injury. Familial rejection increases suicide attempts by as much as eight times more than LGBTQ+ teens who reported no or low levels of familial rejection. If you notice your LGBTQ+ teen displaying any signs of risk, seek professional support immediately.

Juan and Elena

Juan is a parent of a 15-year-old questioning teen by the name of Elena. Elena has been sleeping in a lot more and spending more time alone. She used to perform well at school, but in the last six weeks Juan has noticed her grades slipping.

Suspicion of suicidal thoughts in your child is extremely frightening and is a delicate conversation to broach. The following is an example of how a parent could handle this concern.

Juan: Elena, can I speak with you?

Elena: Sure, what's up, Dad?

Juan: I'm worried about you, honey. I've noticed you haven't been hanging out with the family and your friends as much. You sleep a lot more, and your grades have been slipping. You just haven't been yourself lately.

Elena: I'm fine, Dad.

Juan: This is really hard for me to ask, but I want to ask you if you are having thoughts about harming yourself?

Elena: What do you mean?

Juan: I realize things have been tough since you have been exploring things. I'm asking if you are currently having feelings or thoughts about not living anymore.

Elena: (*silence*)

Juan: I want you to know I'm here for you, and if you were ever feeling like you didn't want to live any more, you could tell me or Mom and we will get you help.

Elena: It's been hard, but you don't have to worry. I'm not feeling like hurting myself or ending my life. I promise I will talk to you or Mom. Promise.

Juan: I love you and would never want you to feel so badly that ending your life seemed like the only option. You know I am here for you and will get you whatever help you need.

If a teen is suicidal, it can make a world of difference to simply know someone cares and is paying attention. It's always better to lean on the side of caution.

SEX AND RELATIONSHIPS

Conversations about sex and relationships are uncomfortable for both parents and LGBTQ+ teens, but they are essential if you want your teen to make choices that are healthy and safe for both their body and their heart. Your discomfort could be a result of feeling isolated yourself, or a of lack of knowledge about LGBTQ+ sexual activity and relationship concerns. I encourage you and your teen to recognize the awkwardness you might both feel and to keep an open and honest approach, along with a willingness to learn together. Remember knowledge is power, and educating your teen about healthy sexual and relationship habits will empower them to make safer choices.

SAFER SEX

Safer sex is still a conversation topic many parents do not relish discussing with their teen, but creating opportunities to talk about STIs (sexually transmitted infections) and pregnancy are critically necessary. These conversations don't have to take place in one sitting, but can occur in small, digestible pieces over time.

Having safer sex conversations with your teen gives them the necessary information and tools to make informed decisions when and if they decide to engage in any type of sexual activity. This is especially important because in many schools, LGBTQ+ health and sex education are not even addressed. The goal is to support your teen to protect themself and increase their chances of experiencing healthier sexual relationships.

PORN

During a time when pornography is so easily accessible, it is even more critical for parents to talk with their teens about pornography literacy. Many LGBTQ+ teens might feel they have nowhere to go or no one to talk to about LGBTQ+ sex–related topics. This often leads teens toward pornography, where they risk learning and developing unrealistic and distorted ideas about sexual behaviors and sexual relationships. For some, this can turn into an addictive habit. I encourage parents to talk with their teens about the risks of exposure to pornography and help them understand healthier and more realistic sexual expectations of themselves and others.

NAVIGATING GENDER IDENTITY

Gender identity can be difficult and confusing for many parents to understand, and I encourage you to remain supportive as your teen tries to figure it out for themself. A common struggle experienced by some transgender teens is gender dysphoria, which is when one's sex assigned at birth does not match one's gender identity, resulting in psychological distress. The individual feels an overwhelming realization that they are of another gender, often feeling their body is wrong. They will generally explore efforts to change their secondary sex characteristics (e.g., hair, appearance of chest) and maybe their primary sex characteristics (e.g., genitals).

GENDER EXPRESSION

Gender expression is what your teen shows to the outside world—how they dress, how they talk, hairstyle, mannerisms, makeup, and what name they want to be called and which pronouns they associate with. Gender expression is often related to gender identity, but they do not necessarily have to align. Gender expression starts developing early and can be observed in children as young as two or three years of age. For some, gender expression can be fluid and change over time. I encourage you to support your child's experimentation and exploration. This will help your teen get the clarity they long for.

USING THE CORRECT PRONOUNS

For a very a long time, LGBTQ+ populations were limited to conventional pronouns like *he* and *she*. However, out of recognition and respect for the diverse identities of LGBTQ+ individuals, we have come to recognize how important and affirming it is to be referenced correctly, and now include gender-neutral pronouns such as *they/them* and *ze/zir*. When an LGBTQ+ person's pronouns are referenced incorrectly, it creates an uncomfortable, distressing, hurtful, and anxiety-provoking experience for them. For parents, family, and friends, this can be a confusing change and will take some time and conscious effort. Being supportive means making an observable effort to acknowledge their identity accurately, and apologizing when you get it wrong. It is also important for parents to advocate for their LGBTQ+ teen and help others who are struggling with getting the pronouns and new name right.

NAME CHANGES

Depending on where you live, a legal name change can be an extremely confusing, difficult, and an expensive process that can take years, but it is a monumental feat and step toward finally being recognized. Transgender individuals have to constantly deal with obstacles anytime an official identification is required, while others on the LGBTQ+ spectrum can easily obtain and use a government-issued identification card that matches their true identity. Even if your LGBTQ+ teen's name change isn't yet official in any legal sense, it is important to use their chosen name and to refrain from calling them by their "dead" name, as this is incredibly hurtful and invalidating.

SOCIAL PRESSURES

LGBTQ+ teens have their own unique sets of social pressures in addition to those all teens face. They may struggle with gender-expression norms, worrying if they appear too flamboyant or too butch. Within the LGBTQ+ community, fitness culture can fuel insecurities about body image. There may be pressures to fit into the party culture, where drinking, drugs, and casual sex are often common. It can be difficult for LGBTQ+ teens to find authentic connections and community.

LACK OF POSITIVE REPRESENTATION IN MEDIA AND POP CULTURE

Although there has been increasingly more LGBTQ+ representation in various media outlets and pop culture over the last few decades, there is still room for more diversity and inclusion of positive LGBTQ+ presences, especially of LGBTQ+ teens of color. Teens are looking for representation they can relate to, that gives them a sense of aspiration and hope for a world they can be part of. Too often, when they do see representations of themselves, it is in harmful stereotypes or tragic and traumatic stories.

NAVIGATING ONLINE CULTURE

The online world presents opportunities for parents to learn about LGBTQ+ teen culture, and it can also be a lens into their world. You and your LGBTQ+ teen can find connections and online communities that will help you both feel less alone, especially if you are in a remote or rural area. However, online culture can also be the place of potential harm. I encourage parents to speak with their teens about what social media platforms and applications they use. Ask them about their experiences, what groups they are a part of, and who they are in communication with, and invite them to share about both positive and negative experiences they have had. How did they handle those negative situations? Do they need your help? Use this as another way to connect with your teen.

Quick Self-Care Tips for Difficult Conversations

Self-care isn't just about eating healthy and occasionally treating yourself to a massage, it's also about how you show care and respect for yourself in any given moment. This can be a tremendously helpful concept to keep in mind when initiating or having a difficult conversation. Take the time to plan and think about how to best execute your conversation, what your goal is, and what the message is that you want your teen to hear from you. Effective communication is more than just an exchange of words; it is also about physical space, facial expressions, and the tone of your voice. Timing is also a key factor—are you in a rush to get to work, did you get enough sleep the night before, are you hungry? The following are a few communication self-care tips I hope you will find helpful.

Know your physical boundaries – Each and every one of us has our "bubble," or our own level of comfort in terms of physical space. You sit down first and then ask your teen to sit where they are most comfortable.

Agree to disagree – Remember your goal is understanding, not necessarily agreement or compliance.

Check in – If the conversation is getting heated or if your teen is no longer hearing you, check in with them and ask if they are all right with continuing the conversation.

Establish rules – It can be helpful to set some boundaries before starting a difficult conversation.

At the End of the Day, Trust Yourself to Know Your Teen

In all my years of working with parents and families, I have learned that many of the challenges parents face are rooted in their own painful life experiences and their own feelings of inadequacy. The critical voice in your head is on replay—"I'm an awful parent," "I must be the worst parent on earth," or "I can't do anything right with my teen; all we do is fight." It's easy to doubt yourself, and you start to think "I don't know my teen anymore" and "I don't know what I am doing." You are not alone, and you are not the only parent who has experienced moments of self-doubt.

Know it is because you do care and love your teen that you are questioning yourself. You want them to be happy and safe, and you desire only the best for them. Take a moment to say something kind to yourself, such as "I am loving my teen the best way I know how." Now repeat it several more times. Do this every day; on some days, you may need to do it several times. Listen to what your heart is telling you. You know your teen better than you think.

Make Them Feel Safe and Heard

I don't know any parent who looks forward to having a difficult conversation with their teen. Know it is hard because you care and are invested in your LGBTQ+ teen's well-being. If you want to be heard and have a connection with your teen, then begin by showing them your respect and sincere desire to listen. Start by asking them how they are doing. Ask them what you can do to help. Put your arms around them and just hold them. You are responsible for letting them know you are in their corner and will keep them safe.

When we feel safe and secure, we feel as though we can breathe easy, even when our world is crumbling and completely chaotic. I tell parents in my therapy room to sit in silence next to their teenager, even when they don't know what to say or how to help. Just your presence and a simple loving gaze, without a word being said, can be very supportive. Leave your child a little note or send them a text saying "I'm here for you," "I'm thinking of you," or "I believe in you."

Conclusion

This chapter may have been a lot for you to digest, and perhaps many of the concepts were new and unfamiliar. I commend you for making it through and showing your willingness to under-stand and support your LGBTQ+ teen. In this chapter, I tried to present the different aspects of LGBTQ+ teen life and the various situations and risks teens can encounter. I also wanted to give you some considerations to think about and tools to help you initiate difficult conversations with your teen. There will be times when you end a conversation and you feel great, and other times when you are left feeling defeated. Remember these conversations are hard, and they will often require more than just one sitting to resolve and figure out. As long as you continue to show up for your teen, over time you will feel closer, gain clarity, and feel more confident about working collaboratively through whatever challenges come your way.

"Perhaps the most important thing we ever give each other is our attention . . . . A loving silence often has far more power to heal and to connect than the most well-intentioned words."

—*Rachel Naomi Remen*

CHAPTER FIVE

Nurture Your Connection

In this chapter, we will look at how you can continue shaping and connecting with your LGBTQ+ teen. In many ways, you are starting all over. One of the struggles I often see parents facing is they can get caught up in their own personal life challenges and, as a result, forget that relationships of all types require ongoing investment and willingness to change. The closeness, connection, and healthy attachment you are seeking does not come from autopilot parenting or doing things exactly the way you've done them in the past. It comes from being able to grow and develop through the different stages of your relationship as your child grows and develops—which includes being uncomfortable and scared at times. Maybe your teen just came out to you and it served as a huge wake-up call. So what happens now? The great news is you have a wonderful opportunity to create a new and improved connection with your teen.

Maria and Carlos

Maria and Carlos have been married for twenty-one years. They have two daughters and a son, ranging in ages from 4 to 15. Their son, Miguel, is 15 years old and recently came out to them as gay.

87

Maria used to have a much closer relationship with Miguel, but since he came out, she is struggling to make sense of how she ended up having a gay son. Growing up in Colombia during the late 1980s, Maria was raised a devout Catholic and continues to attend Sunday mass regularly. She feels worried and sad all the time thinking that Miguel won't have the life she envisioned for him. Carlos, on the other hand, is a third-generation Mexican American from a less religious background and is more accepting of Miguel's sexual orientation. Maria has a large extended group of family and friends nearby, but she doesn't feel comfortable speaking with them and often feels very alone and isolated. Maria sought support through therapy. Over the course of several months of weekly therapy, Maria came to understand her reactions and became more aware of how to better support Miguel. Carlos and Miguel attended several sessions with Maria where they learned how to improve their communication and manage their feelings better. They learned how to listen to one another and at least try to better understand one another, even if they might not agree on everything. Things are not perfect by any means, but they have agreed to continue their family journey with a little more optimism.

No Matter What Happens, You Are Your Teen's Lifeline

You might worry about what you must offer your teen as a parent now that you know they identify as queer: Are you too different from each other now? Will they still "need" you? The truth is you will always be your teen's lifeline; it will just look a bit different than what you were expecting. You may feel a bit lost and uncertain for a while, but regular communication and learning together will help you build your connection. During this time, it's important to keep the faith and simply be there for them.

The key is to focus on what you both share and build from there. While there will still be bumps in the road, continue to keep your hands on the steering wheel for you and your teen. As your teen experiments and explores, there will be difficult and challenging moments for them. They might experience their first breakup, and will need your care and support to guide them through it. Your teen will encounter other new situations they have never faced before, and you want them to know they can come to you for advice on how to deal with it, or simply for a shoulder to cry on.

Your Teen Will Teach You as Much as You Teach Them

Many parents still lean toward a more conventional or authoritative style of parenting that favors a strict hierarchy of power where knowledge can pass only from the top down. However, if your goal is to have a relationship of reciprocal growing with your teen, you'll want to embrace a different approach. As your teen's lifeline and safety, consider instead that you are working on the same team to build each other up and help each other thrive.

Make a conscious effort to spend one-on-one time with your teen and to learn about what is going on with them, including things specific to their LGBTQ+ life. Focus on who they are today—not who they were in the past or who you think they should be. You might be curious about what their LGBTQ+ experience has been like so far, who their role models are, or if there is anyone at school they have a crush on—so ask them! Show interest in their social circles and convey a welcoming message to their friends so you can learn about the important people in their life outside the home. Taking these consistent, proactive steps will help strengthen your connection over time.

Find Common Ground

When parents mention struggling to connect with their LGBTQ+ teen, I often encourage them to think about common ground they already share. Just because your teen came out as LGBTQ+ doesn't mean the meaningful ways in which you connected before no longer exist in your relationship. The following are some ways you can find and nurture the common ground you have with your teen:

Connect with yourself – Spend some time understanding your own needs to connect and how you prefer to connect.

Rediscover your teen – Learn about them as if you are meeting for the first time. Be curious and observe.

Accept them – Let them know you love and will continue to love them just as they are.

Notice the positives – Leave them a note, send a text, or just take a moment to tell them you noticed their success—they were on time, they did something without being asked, they made an effort to get along with a sibling, etc.

Collaborate on a solution – When issues come up, work with your teen to figure out an agreeable solution. Hear them out, and they will feel recognized and respected by you, and they will have buy-in to the solution.

Seek Out Activities That Bring You Closer Together

The simplest of activities can help nurture more closeness with your teen. What are some existing activities or interests your family enjoys together? What are some of the rituals, celebrations, and traditions important to you and your LGBTQ+ teen?

Asking your teen for their ideas allows them to feel they have some say, and they will be more inclined to participate as a result.

The following are some simple ways you can connect with your teen:

- Cooking a meal together
- Redecorating their room together
- Going to an LGBTQ+-sponsored event together
- Going on a walk together
- Sitting together and having them share their latest favorite app or music with you

It is important to keep in mind that you, your spouse or partner, your teen, and other immediate family members might be at a different level of acceptance and comfort than you. Do what feels right for you and be patient with the readiness of others. If, for example, your LGBTQ+ teen is not ready to join in on any connecting activities, then it is best not to push or force them to do anything. Let them know it is okay and when they are ready, you would like to spend more time together.

A List of Positive LGBTQ+ Movies, TV Shows, and Novels

Many LGBTQ+ teens are trying to figure out what it means to identify as LGBTQ+, and they are also desperately trying to figure out how they fit into the straight world. It can be difficult to imagine who you could be if you have no role models or significant figures to identify with. Although this is not an exhaustive list, here are some noteworthy movies, TV shows, and novels that can offer some ideas of what the LGBTQ+ experience and life could look like:

Movies – *Alex Strangelove; Beautiful Thing; Beginners; Boy Erased; But I'm a Cheerleader; Edge of Seventeen; The Feels; G.B.F.; The Half of It; The Incredibly True Adventures of Two Girls in Love; Love, Simon; Pariah; The Perks of Being a Wallflower; Transamerica*

TV Shows – *Elite; Glee; I Am Jazz; The L Word; The L Word: Generation Q; Love, Victor; Modern Family; One Day at a Time; Pose; Queer as Folk; Queer Eye; RuPaul's Drag Race; Schitt's Creek; Will & Grace; Vida; Dear White People; Brooklyn Nine-Nine; Euphoria*

Novels – *Aristotle and Dante Discover the Secrets of the Universe,* by Benjamin Alire Sáenz; *Georgia Peaches and Other Forbidden Fruit,* by Jaye Robin Brown; *I Wish You All the Best,* by Mason Deaver; *If I Was Your Girl,* by Meredith Russo; *Last Night at the Telegraph Club,* by Melinda Lo; *Little & Lion,* by Brandy Colbert; *Two Boys Kissing,* by David Levithan; *We Are the Ants,* by Shaun David Hutchinson; *You Should See Me in a Crown,* by Leah Johnson

Build Trust

As a parent, having trust between you and your teen is an important building block of a healthy and growing relationship. Teens want to be trusted and feel trustworthy, and that trust starts with you. Throughout their childhood, they trusted you to keep them safe and take care of them. Now, as teens, they still want those things, and they need you to practice what you preach. It may be time for you to ask yourself if you are modeling the same expectations you have of them.

As you continue to create and maintain a trusting connection with your teen, it's important to stay consistent. Your teen might already be questioning the idea of trust, not just with you, but also in other aspects of their life—with their friends, teachers, therapist, doctor, and others who have previously told them "I am here for you" but then disappoint in some way. When people in our lives are not consistent, it makes us question if we can truly trust them. So when you say you are going to do something for them or with them, do it.

If your teen has already come out to you, it's a huge confirmation you have already built some trust. They have communicated "I am trusting you" through their choice to come out to you. You can reassure your teen of that trust by letting them know you will respect their privacy by not sharing their sexual orientation and gender identity with others without asking them if it is okay first. Keep in mind many teens worry about being outed and the potential consequences.

Earn Their Respect

Earning someone's respect takes time, ongoing consistency, and observable effort. Sometimes we react in ways we are not proud of because we feel we are not being heard or seen, or because we're afraid—but that's no excuse. If you want your teen to respect you, then you must be willing to consistently show them the same respect. When you make a mistake, own it. That is the first step to repairing any damage that might have been caused.

I also want to acknowledge the importance of respecting yourself. Over the years, your teen has learned what respect looks like by watching how you treat yourself and others. Respecting yourself means recognizing your own needs for self-care by taking a time-out to sort through your overwhelming emotions, being clear about your own boundaries, and forgiving yourself for making mistakes. Another way to respect yourself is by surrounding yourself with positive influences, such as close friends and family, who can remind you of your worth. When your teen sees you respecting yourself and others, they are also learning how to value and respect themself.

Check in Often

Checking in often and regularly is a way you can communicate to your teen you are paying attention and you care, and it reminds them they are not alone. It is a great way to keep a finger on the pulse of how your teen is doing and to be aware of any red flags, needs, or concerns your teen might be dealing with. Check-ins don't always have to be formal, such as a scheduled meeting at the kitchen table. Keeping things low-key, short, and simple often works best for teens, such as popping into their room and asking them what interesting thing happened in their day or what's the latest app they've been using. Other ways don't even require their involvement but are more observational: How are they caring for their personal appearance? How late are they staying up at night because of homework or being on their electronic devices? Have there been any changes to their social and extra-curricular life? Try on different ways to check in and see what they respond to the best.

WHAT IS YOUR TEEN REALLY FEELING?

Who would have thought recognizing and naming our feelings could be so hard? We often use abstract terms such as *depressed* or *anxious*. However, there is a wide range of emotions beyond these, and you can help your teen figure things out if they are having a hard time naming their emotions. Let them know all feelings are okay—and often necessary—to have, even the painful and sad ones. This is an emotional time for you, too, full of different feelings that can change from one moment to the next. You can also use this as an opportunity to share your own feelings and talk with your teen about how you are managing them.

Stay Informed

There are new changes going on constantly in the LGBTQ+ world, so you may not always be able to keep up, but it is tremendously helpful for parents to do their best to stay informed on current events, legislation, and other issues impacting the LGBTQ+ community. It can be an important way to connect with your teenager and can also give you greater insight into the issues your teen might be dealing with or worrying about. Talk with your teen about what LGBTQ+ interests and new discoveries they are currently active in: social apps, artists, groups at school or online. Do your own research and get involved in politics in your community, Pride events, your teen's school PTA, or PFLAG (Parents, Families, and Friends of Lesbians and Gays).

ACTIVE LISTENING EXERCISE

One of the challenges that makes it difficult for parents to connect with their teens is a lack of listening to one another. This exercise not only helps develop listening skills, but it also establishes a commitment to making time for each other. As a listener, pay attention to your nonverbal communication (nods, facial expression, body language) and what messages it may be sending to your teen.

1. Find a place that is private and quiet and where you both feel comfortable.

2. Set a timer (such as the one on your smartphone) for 3 minutes to start. The time can later be extended to up to 5 minutes as you both get better at listening.

3. For the agreed-upon time, one person speaks about anything they want to. This can be about school, relationships, an unresolved topic, any new interests, and so on.

4. The person who is listening simply listens to what the speaker is sharing, without interrupting or offering an opinion.

5. When the person is done speaking, the listener will repeat back what they heard. Do not provide any commentary, judgment, or reaction—just summarize. When done, ask the speaker if you got everything or if anything was missed.

6. The speaker can respond briefly to fill in anything the listener missed.

7. Now switch roles and repeat.

Be Open—Especially When It's Not Easy for You

When we feel scared and uncertain, we might be inclined to close ourselves off. We put up our defenses or crawl back into our shells. No one likes feeling vulnerable, but this is also the time we have the most potential to show our courage and grow. Even when it's hard, you need to rise to the occasion and remain open to your LGBTQ+ teen. By being open, you are practicing an attitude of curiosity rather than judgment. You are establishing a connection with your teen and showing them you respect their individuality. You are showing them you value seeing things from different vantage points so you may have a better view of the bigger picture. When we are open, we are less rigid, which allows us to be kinder and more compassionate with ourselves and others when we make mistakes, and our imperfections feel less threatening.

Have Conversations That Don't Revolve Around Discipline or Rules

When things feel out of sync, it is so easy to get mentally and emotionally hijacked by worry and the desire to be in control. But it's important to continue to communicate and connect with your teen in many ways, and not just via enforcing rules and expectations.

Try engaging your teen in a conversation about their hopes and dreams, or new things they have discovered. LGBTQ+ teens are still teenagers who have celebrity and peer crushes, favorite TV shows and characters, a new favorite music artist, and the latest phone app they are into. Have fun, laugh, and learn about your teen. There is so much to discover about each other.

If you have been struggling with your teen's identity and your relationship has been feeling strained, one way you can try to connect with your LGBTQ+ teen is to talk about happy memories. Being able to dig deep and reach for more pleasant memories that anchor your relationship is a strategy to evoke positive emotions, remind you both how important you are to each other, and start healing. You can remind yourselves it's not all bad and you do in fact have a strong relationship foundation to build upon.

When You Disagree, Make It a Learning Opportunity

You and your LGBTQ+ teen are not always going to agree about everything, but you can deepen your relationship by trying to understand each other more. Your teen is going to start exploring, experimenting, and developing their own thoughts and opinions about their life, who they are, who they want to be, what they like, what they don't like—the list goes on and on. This is a good thing!

Parents sometimes make the mistake of interpreting their teen's disagreement as an intentional act of disrespect. But please keep in mind one of the healthiest skills that will benefit your teen and their future is learning how to think critically for themself and to feel confident in their beliefs. I invite you to look at disagreements as a learning opportunity. Ask questions. Try to understand how they arrived at their point of view and encourage them to ask you questions in return. You are teaching and modeling for your teen that in this world, there will be people whose values and opinions differ from ours, but it is possible to get along with others and stay true to our convictions. You are teaching your teen that making the effort to understand another person, even if you disagree, has value. You are showing them you can respect them and their thoughts, even though you might not completely understand or agree with them.

What About Discipline?

Discipline shapes how teens will behave within limits that are agreeable and set by both of you. By providing clear guidelines about what is and isn't acceptable within your home, you are helping your teen mature and figure out how to be independent. The goal is for your teen to learn their own limits and self-discipline. You are teaching them to take personal responsibility for their choices, and that their behaviors have consequences. It is worth pointing out your teen does not yet possess the brain development and skills to make all their own decisions. Those parts of their brain won't fully develop until they are in their midtwenties.

Allowing your teen to have room to make mistakes and learn about the consequences of their decisions will assist them in developing self-control and self-regulation. Like so many parts of parenting, consistency is key. Supporting your teen through proper use of discipline will help them be responsible and self-disciplined young adults. And even though they might sometimes not like the consequences of their choices and decisions, you are creating a solid relationship that supports a sense of freedom, clear boundaries, and safety between you and them.

DON'T EVER MAKE IT ABOUT WHO THEY ARE

It is important to remember your LGBTQ+ teen may already be experiencing feelings of shame, guilt, and inadequacy related to their sexual orientation and gender identity. When you talk to them about any of their behaviors causing a strong reaction in you, it is important to not make it a personal attack on who they are, or their LGBTQ+ identity. You can help them by focusing specifically on their behaviors. For example, "I don't appreciate you being dishonest with me about where you were last night" is better than, "What is wrong with you? You're such a liar," or, "Is this what it's going to be like now that you've come out? Always lying to me?" These types of personal attacks will continue to degrade their sense of self.

BE KIND BUT FIRM

Setting loving and fair limits is a difficult balance for a lot of parents. You can be clear about your rules and expectations without yelling, cursing, or shaming. When parents start expressing themselves in unkind and hurtful ways, the message gets lost because your teen feels attacked and gets defensive. A good rule is if you are feeling too upset to speak calmly, take a time-out for yourself. Tell your teen their behavior is not acceptable, you are upset, and you will be talking to them later after you cool down.

SET CLEAR EXPECTATIONS

Teens function best when you are clear about your expectations and boundaries. I cannot emphasize enough how important it is for parent to be consistent, fair, and transparent about the rules. Teens need to know there will be specific consequences if they act out or behave in a particular manner.

FOLLOW THROUGH

Consistency provides your teen with structure, safety, trust, security, and stability. When you do not follow through, you are hurting your teen and you are also hurting yourself. You are giving your teen the message they cannot depend on you, and they will lose faith and trust in you. By staying firm and consistent with your boundaries and promises, you are modeling for your teen that keeping your word matters, making it more likely they, too, will grow up to be a person who keeps their promises and has strong boundaries.

Your LGBTQ+ teen will undoubtedly behave in ways that are not acceptable and require some form of discipline. The following is an example of how you could handle a situation with your teen who snuck out of the house and came home drunk.

Parent: Young lady, do you know what time it is? I have been worried sick about you!

Teen: Can we not deal with this right now? I don't feel good.

Parent: Go to your room. But we will be talking about this tomorrow.

(Next day, midmorning)

Parent: Morning. How are you feeling?

Teen: Can you please stop yelling? My head hurts.

Parent: *(In a calm voice)* That's called a hangover. And I'm not yelling at you.

Teen: Can you make me something to eat?

Parent: You can do that yourself.

Teen: But I don't feel well.

Parent: I am not the one who decided to sneak out. You are always telling me you are not a child anymore.

Teen: Ugh.

Parent: So where did you go last night? I worry when it's late and I don't know where you are. You can't just leave the house any time you want to, especially when you are already on restriction.

Teen: I was with my friend Tiffany. She was having a party. I had to be there. Everyone was going.

Parent: I get that you wanted to go, but you know the rules. Now your restriction will get extended by a week.

Teen: But why?

Parent: You snuck out of the house. When you break rules, there are consequences. You know that.

Teen: But, Dad.

Parent: You did this by the choice you made when you snuck out. You know better.

Teen: (*Storms off and goes to their room*)

Parent: (*Doesn't chase after teen and allows some time for them to both cool off*)

Managing Aggression or Violent Outbursts

In the unfortunate situation where your teen may show aggression or even violence, it is important to first prioritize the safety of your teen, your other family members, and yourself. *Everyone needs to take a time-out!* Acknowledge your teen is feeling angry and upset, then in a firm but calm voice direct them to stop what they are doing and go try to calm down. Give them some space. If you are unable to stay calm and in control of the situation, and you have a partner or spouse, ask for them to take over. Let your teen know you are going to give them 10 minutes and then you are going to make sure they are okay. Check in on them when you said you would. They might tell you they are still angry or upset. If this is the case, give them more time. The worst thing you can do is to force a conversation or consequence when emotions are running high. When you and your teen are calm, then ask them if you can talk about what happened and what they need so that does not happen again.

Your teen may not completely understand why they became so aggressive and violent. Extreme emotional states could be indicators of so many different things—maybe something happened at school, maybe they are dealing with something said about them on social media, or maybe they are in some type of emotional pain and suffering and do not have the cognitive ability or tools to manage whatever it is they are going through. Let your teen know that, no matter what they are going through, you are still there and would like to help them. If this is an ongoing problem and you fear for the safety of your teen, yourself, or your family, I strongly recommend seeking professional help.

When I Came Out, My Parent Was . . .

When we are going through a lot of emotions and challenges in our lives, it can be easy to forget the type of parent we want to be. It can be helpful for you to spend some time thinking about what you would like for your LGBTQ+ teen to say about their experience when they first came out. Here are some points to consider:

- My teen knew I loved them by . . .
- I supported my teen to prepare for adulthood when . . .
- In what ways did I help others accept my teen?
- How did I react when they told me they were LGBTQ+?
- When they were going through a rough time, how did I help?
- I showed my acceptance of my teen by . . .
- I encouraged my teen to explore by . . .

Help Build Their Character

Character is the foundation of who your teenager is at their core. It can be helpful to think of character as both how we act out our values and how we behave when no one else is watching. This can be especially difficult for your teen because they spend so much time worrying about how they appear to their peers. When your teen has a strong foundation of character based on courage, resilience, fortitude, honesty, and loyalty, it will help them face life's challenges and minimize the negative influences they might encounter.

Engage in conversations with your teen about their values and what is important to them. Show by example that you are someone whose actions align with your values. Ask them what challenges they face and how they cope with those challenges. Character is developed and refined over time, through experiences and challenges your teen has and will continue to face, and when they make their own decisions and accept the consequences of their decisions.

Give Them Your Undivided Attention

In our fast-paced lives, it can feel impossible to try to balance our family life, our own self-care, friends, work, community involvement, and other day-to-day demands. You feel pulled in many different directions, and it can be easy to get overwhelmed and distracted. The challenge is that you have a teenager who needs you. When they come to you for help, or when you are simply spending time with them, try as best as you can to give them your undivided attention. They need to know you care about them and what they have to say.

Part of creating a close connection requires our full focus, because otherwise very important details get missed. If the timing is bad, let your teen know you are busy, but make an effort to commit to connecting with them at a later time—and stick to that commitment. When you are together, be intentional and put aside your cell phone, tablet, or dishrag; turn off the television; and close your laptop. When your teen is talking, face them and give them your eye contact, and allow them to speak completely before interjecting or offering up your thoughts and opinions.

Let Them Know You Love Them No Matter What

Many LGBTQ+ teens struggle with feelings of inadequacy and need assurance they are loved. I have yet to meet a teenager in my therapy room who doesn't long for a connection with their parent—even when they act like they do not. Sometimes it is the simple things that have the most profound effect. Just sending a lighthearted text once in a while can let them know you are thinking about them. Letting them pick the music in the car sends the message you care about their interests and helps them feel included. Most importantly, recognize and love them for who they are. Learn about what is important to them and let them know you are proud of them for accomplishing what is important to *them*, not necessarily what is important to you. When you are upset with them, make it clear you still, and always will, love them—no matter what.

MY PARENTAL GOALS

There was no roadmap for parenting your young child, and you might feel even more lost parenting your LGBTQ+ teenager. It is up to you to create your own goals as a parent and to be clear about the expectations you have for yourself. If you do not have a clear vision of the kind of parent you want to be, it can be easy to lose focus on what is truly important. This exercise can help you stay focused whenever you feel overwhelmed and unsure as a parent.

1. Take a piece of paper and pen and find a quiet place where you won't be bothered.

2. Brainstorm a list of ideas you have about what is going to make you feel successful as a parent. What are your values as a parent? What does being a parent mean to you?

3. When you are done, review the list and pick one to three goals that stand out the most.

4. On a separate piece of paper, come up with several ideas for how you can achieve each of these goals.

5. When you are done, keep these lists in a safe place. If you want, you can share with your spouse or partner. Whenever you feel lost or unsure, refer to this list. Over time, the list can change. Consider it a living document that can be revised and changed as needed.

Conclusion

This chapter was about deepening your connection with your LGBTQ+ teen. It is also about recognizing your ongoing value and worth to your teen. Even though they are becoming more independent, you are still their parent and one of the most influential people in their life. Being able to define and redefine your parental role is part of your journey. Your success nurturing your connection with your teen demands that you explore and embrace some new ways of being a parent. Keeping yourself open to new shared experiences, setting much-needed boundaries, and allowing room for you and your teen to grow together are some of the key messages I want for you to take from this chapter. Now let's continue to the next chapter and explore how to further support your LGBTQ+ teen in their growing exploration of self.

"Be more concerned with your character than your reputation, because your character is what you really are, while your reputation is merely what others think you are."

—John Wooden

CHAPTER SIX

Empower Your Teen to Be Who They Are

The reality is that your LGBTQ+ teen will continue to face challenging and difficult situations for the rest of their life because of their sexual orientation and gender identity, and you will not always be around or available to help them fix things—nor do I believe this is what you want. It has been my observation that helicopter parents do their teens a huge disservice, as well-intentioned as they might be. So how do you empower your teen to be their honest, confident, caring, trustworthy, and resilient self? This chapter is going to address ways you can help your teen embrace their strengths and continue to develop emotionally, mentally, spiritually, and socially as they grow into healthy and competent young adults.

Derek and Sam

Derek is the father of a 13-year-old whom he and his wife named Samantha as a baby, but who now prefers to be called Sam. For years, Sam told his father and mother he wants to be like his brother. Sam regularly binds his chest, which has caused him immense pain, but he says the pain is worth it. Since Sam was in his toddler years, he has had increasing fits of anger and physical self-harm. Sam's parents are moderately conventional in their views, and Sam's assertion he is a boy has caused many blow-ups in their family. They know a few people who are LGBTQ+, but they were brought up traditionally Chinese and Catholic and don't quite understand the transgender identity. After years of Sam seeing therapists, psychiatrists, and medical professionals, they have decided to explore puberty blockers. They learned about the importance of how to safely chest-bind to prevent any dangerous harm. They also were educated about top (chest) surgery, as an option for when Sam is older. It took Sam's parents a long time to make a decision, but with Sam's persistence, support from their local PFLAG group, and active monitoring with medical and mental health professionals, Sam has started the puberty blockers. This has not been an easy journey for Sam's family, but his parents are amazed at the changes Sam has made emotionally, academically, and socially in just over a year's time since starting the blockers. Sam is thriving, and the family is continuing their work on connecting and healing.

Your LGBTQ+ Teen Needs Your Support

One of the reasons you picked up this book is because you want to be a more supportive parent to your LGBTQ+ teen, which is critical to your teen's healthy development. Your support will help them strengthen their self-esteem, facilitate better self-care and decision-making, and fortify family relationships. Being supportive can look a lot of different ways and take many different forms, and the needs for support are unique to every teenager.

One way to be supportive is to encourage your LGBTQ+ teen to explore their sexuality and gender identity. It is important for them to understand what it means to them to be LGBTQ+ and to discover how to be their authentic, LGBTQ+ self. Listening is also one of the most important ways you can be a supportive parent. Really try to hear them as they share the challenges they are facing in different areas of their life. Ask them directly how they want you to support them. Cheer for their successes and allow them to make mistakes and face their challenges. Establish structure and security with clear expectations and consequences. Above all, the ultimate support factor is trust.

For transgender boys or young men, it is important to know chest binding is often used to minimize the appearance of breasts, and this is okay, if done safely. Be sure your teen uses binders made specifically for chests. It is unsafe to use home remedies such Ace bandages, which can cause permanent harm such that top surgery is no longer an option. In addition, binders should not be used for longer than eight hours. Support informed and safe chest binding practices.

Boost Their Self-Esteem

Self-esteem is about acceptance, valuing ourselves, and liking who we are. It is an internal or mental measure of how we fit into the world around us. Too often, teens will connect their self-esteem to choices and pursuits they believe will make them more accepted and loveable to others, instead of focusing on themselves. As a parent, you can help gently guide your teen away from seeking self-esteem and validation primarily through the lens of others—peers, school, parents, and family—and help them move toward prioritizing doing things out of love and care for themself.

A good place to start is with taking a moment to think about how you feed into your LGBTQ+ teen's self-confidence—or lack there of. Could there be things you have said or done to your teen, in the past or currently, you need to change? Have you reacted to them in ways that might have caused them to feel shame or lack of acceptance? Of course, your role as a parent is to guide your teen away from decisions or interests that could bring them harm; what is important is being aware of how you are delivering your message. The message you want your teen to receive is they are valued and their ideas, whatever they may be, are important. Encourage and support them to make better decisions that strengthen their love of self. It can be as simple as asking, "Is this a decision that's going to make you feel good about yourself?"

Build Their Self-Worth

Self-worth is a term often confused or used interchangeably with *self-esteem*, but there is an important difference. When I am talking about building self-worth within your LGBTQ+ teen, I am talking about the degree to which they believe in their ability, effort, and performance. LGBTQ+ teens often feel inadequate in at least one if not all these areas, but as their parent, you have the ability to help your teen develop a healthier way of recognizing and owning their strengths.

You can help your teen get better at recognizing their value by emphasizing they are more than what others say about them. Even though they might not get the highest grades in math, didn't get a lot of likes on their recent social media post, or didn't get invited to a peer's party because they are LGBTQ+, they still deserve to be happy, loved, and feel good about who they are. Encourage them to love who they are rather than what they are able to do, and give praise based on their effort and enthusiasm rather than focusing solely on grades, awards, or other arbitrary markers of success. When you love your teen for who they are, you are teaching them how to love themself just as they are.

Mood Swings

The following is a conversation between a father and his transgender son. They have been having problems getting along ever since Angel started taking testosterone. Mood swings are often reported by transgender boys or young men, especially when they have started testosterone injections.

Parent: Angel, can I talk with you?

Angel: Sure, Dad.

Parent: I've been a bit worried about you.

Angel: What about?

Parent: Well, I have been noticing you've been pretty moody these last couple of months, ever since you started the testosterone shots.

Angel: Are you saying that it's my fault for feeling angry?

Parent: Now hold on, I am not talking about blame. But I have noticed you getting mad at your teachers, your girlfriend, and me. I have noticed some changes in you and I want to make sure you're okay.

Angel: I guess I've been noticing it, too. I don't really know what's going on. All I know is I just want to be a boy so badly.

Parent: I know, son. What do you think about us checking in with your doctor? Maybe they can help.

Angel: Okay.

Parent: Okay? Great! You know I love you, right?

Angel: Yes, Dad. I love you, too.

Parent: I'll call the doctor tomorrow. We will figure out this anger thing together.

Soothe Their Inner Critic

We all have that critical voice inside our heads telling us we're not good enough, we messed up, or there is something wrong with us, but that voice is often even louder and more discouraging for LGBTQ+ teens. The first step in helping your teen quiet that inner critic is by normalizing it for them. Let them know having a critical and negative voice is not unique to them. You can also let them know you want them to tell you if you are ever doing anything to perpetuate their feelings of negativity. The key is not pretending these thoughts don't exist, but helping your teen accept they will arise every now and then, and that they have the power to manage the thoughts rather than being paralyzed by them. One of the most empowering lessons any of us can learn is that we can't always control the thoughts popping into our heads, but we get to choose how we respond to them. A simple but effective practice can be just saying a silent "No, thank you" every time an intrusive and unhelpful thought wants our attention.

Another thing you can do to support your teen is to remind them there are other, positive things about them that are true, besides what their inner critic is telling them. Help them accept and allow compliments to sink in. Often, when we receive positive accolades, we tend to minimize or deflect them. If your teen is doing this, let them know it's okay to accept compliments and own their achievements.

Silencing Creeping Negative Thoughts

Persistent negative and critical thoughts can be distracting and can put us in a headspace less than compassionate toward ourselves. I suspect at times you have been hard on yourself about your parenting and your relationship with your LGBTQ+ teen. It can be helpful to simply acknowledge your "stinking thinking" by getting a piece of paper and writing down all the different negative thoughts streaming through your mind that provoke your self-judgment. Then, once you are done, go through your list and think about all the different ways each thought is not true. Find evidence to back up your case with loving acts you have done in the past or positive character traits of your child that can be attributed to how you raised them. It's time to be both honest and kind to yourself. I am sure you will find many examples throughout the years, up through the present day, to discredit your negative thoughts and acknowledge your parental strengths and successes.

Help Them Thrive as Individuals

When I speak about thriving, I am considering a broad perspective on how your LGTBQIA+ teen is growing, developing, and surviving. I am addressing your teen's ability to reach their desired goals and full potential despite challenges they face in the different areas of their lives. This period and their adjustment to their LGBTQ+ identity is a time of vulnerability and evolution. I realize it can be difficult for you to stand by through all the changes, sometimes multiple times in the same day, but I assure you that you are helping them thrive as individuals and it will pay off in the long run.

A critical ingredient for success is safety. When your teen feels safe to pursue their interests and self-exploration, they get better at making decisions that serve them well. It can also be helpful to remind your teen that making mistakes is okay and helps us gain clarity on the things we like and don't like. Embracing the idea that mistakes should be welcomed rather than avoided or feared is a healthy mindset encouraging self-acceptance and growth. Your unconditional love and support will give your teen the approval and acceptance they need to thrive.

Foster Growth

Fostering a growth mindset is when we focus on getting better and improving ourselves—which I'm guessing is what you want for your teen. It does not mean we see who we are and where we are now as bad or not good enough; rather, it acknowledges our lives have potential for change and we want to invest in ourselves to achieve that potential. A growth mindset is also not absent of disappointments or failures. What is important is that when we experience those disappointments, we get up, dust ourselves off, and move forward. Your LGBTQ+ teen may experience moments of doubt and confusion for all sorts of reasons—due to their sexuality and gender identity, or because their peers were cruel and judgmental, for instance. Their journey might bring feelings of sadness and anxiety, and I encourage you to help them work through their emotions.

A growth mindset is not a single destination point, but an attitude one has toward all of life's ups and downs. Your LGBTQ+ teen will go through ongoing growth experiences throughout their life, and I encourage you to begin to instill this skill as early as possible in their developmental years. Your teen is growing and developing in so many different ways—physically, mentally, emotionally, relationally, academically, and socially, just to name a few. You can support your teen by checking in with them and asking how they are doing and what their current challenges and successes are. Ask them how you can help them grow from the experiences they are dealing with.

INSIDE OUT

This is an exercise I often use to help parents understand themselves better. It is also a great exercise for teens. You can even share it with your teen, and vice versa, as an opportunity for you and your teen to learn about each other.

1. Take a piece of paper and lay it out horizontally.

2. Fold the left and right ends so they meet in the middle, like a closed cabinet.

3. On the outside, draw a picture of yourself as you think of yourself, or think others see you, as a parent. Don't worry about being an artist; you can draw a stick figure if that's the best you can do.

4. You can then write out words or draw more pictures or symbols that represent how you and others see you as a parent.

5. Now I want you to open the folds. This is the inside you, the real you. This is who you think your teen does not see or know. Write and draw here words and symbols that represent the real, authentic you.

6. Optional: You can share this with your teen and talk about it with them. If they are open to it, you can do this together or they can also do it alone and share it with you if you choose.

Support Their Experimentation

Supporting your teen's experimentation will likely be a challenge for you. Keep in mind that for your teen to evolve and develop into a healthy, happy, and confident LGBTQ+ young adult, they need to have opportunities to try things out for themself. Of course, if your teen is putting themself in imminent danger, then certainly you must intervene and set boundaries for their safety. But it's important to be honest about why we're afraid. Are they really in danger, or are we just scared because we don't understand?

Your teen is trying to make a statement: "I am no longer a child!" Your job is to keep calm while your teen experiments with a whole slew of ways to express themself: gender expression, sexual orientation, music, fashion, pop culture icons, ambitions, political views, diet, romantic attractions, social groups, interests, cultural connections—the list goes on and on. Try to be curious rather than judgmental about what their current phase is. Ask them about it with an open mind and genuine interest. Ask yourself—and maybe even ask them—how you can support them through their phase. Trust they will figure out who they are and you won't feel as though you are in the middle of a hurricane.

Let Them Take the Lead in Defining Their Experience

It won't be much longer until your teen grows into an independent young adult. I understand your parental, protective urge is wanting to speak out and guide, but this is a reminder to you of how important it is for your teen to develop and strengthen their skills in problem-solving and making independent decisions so they will be able to feel more confident in owning their journey. As much as you may want to, you cannot plan or control the experience your LGBTQ+ teen will have or who they will become. If you try, most likely you will be met with resistance and resentment.

Giving your teen the freedom to take the lead in defining their experience lets your teen know you believe in them and you trust them. This is huge when a teen is feeling ambivalent or unsure of their decision-making and choices. If you want your teen to grow up to be secure and trust their judgment, let them figure it out now while they are still under your roof and watchful eye. The most significant ways we grow and learn are through our own experiences and the natural consequences we must face.

Let Them Choose How They Present Themselves to the World

There are many ways your teen may want to present themself to the world, and these may change repeatedly over the course of their adolescence and young adulthood. Teens already deal with the social pressure of how others think they should be. As part of a healthy development of self, it is important for them to have a say in what makes them feel confident, strong, and reassured, and to love themselves with their heads held high. Remember that the ways teens express themselves can also serve as signals to others in their community and have the potential of forging meaningful connections and community.

When parents do not support or allow teens to present themselves in their own way, teens learn that what others think about them is more important than their own happiness and being their true selves. Unreasonable restrictions can also result in a teen rebelling just to assert their autonomy, sometimes in ways not in their best interest. In some situations, teens may develop emotional and mental health challenges because they feel restricted from being themselves. Ultimately, talking to your teen and encouraging conversations about what self-expression means to them can be an important way to connect and gain insight. You can evaluate the positives and the negatives together, particularly when it comes to permanent expressions involving tattoos, piercings, and earlobe stretching.

CLOTHING

For most teens, what they wear expresses who they are. Unlike their heterosexual and cisgender peers, LGBTQ+ teens have the added pressure of worrying about things such as "Is this too gay?" "Is this too boyish?" "Will this get too much attention and make me unsafe?" and "How will my parents feel about me wearing this?" Clothing is very important to your teen, and although you might not understand their clothing choices, try your best to allow them to dress in ways validating of their self-expression.

HAIR AND MAKEUP

For some LGBTQ+ teens, hair and makeup can be a big part of their self-expression, particularly when it comes to gender expression. Hair and makeup can serve as a protective shield that allows them to feel more confident, and it can be a cathartic way to cope and deal with the LGBTQ+-phobic world. Many LGBTQ+ teens consider hair and makeup to be essential tools in their empowerment and expression of their authentic selves.

Tips on Empowering Your Teenager

Empowering your teen does not have to be complicated. Here are a few quick and easy ways that you can be a cheerleader for your LGBTQ+ teen:

- Give them time to think and come up with solutions to their problems.
- Give them more opportunities to be responsible for themself.
- Acknowledge their strengths and talents.
- Allow them to struggle sometimes. You don't need to always solve their problems.
- Establish clear structure and expectations.
- Hold them accountable to the consequences of their decisions.
- Ask them for their ideas and suggestions.
- Model for them in your behavior the same expectations you have of them.
- Support them by teaching them problem-solving skills.
- Encourage values and integrity.
- Allow them space to discover themself.

Welcome Their Friends into Your Home

At some point, your LGBTQ+ teen is going to want to invite friends over. Being welcoming and inviting other LGBTQ+ teens into your home communicates to your teen your support and validation of them. It is a huge message of love and care for your teen to hear "Your friends are welcome to come over to our home" or "I'd love an opportunity to meet your friends." To help your teen's guests feel welcomed, and to foster warm and considerate interactions, you might consider asking your teen to share with you a little about their friends. Preparing yourself with pronouns or any other helpful details will allow for you to be more comfortable. You may want to be extra mindful and refrain from making gender-specific references such as *boys* or *girls*.

Your LGBTQ+ teen may also want to have a sleepover with friends at some point. Whether at your home or a friend's, this can bring up a whole mix of concerns for parents. My suggestion is to talk with your teen about the friends they would like to have a sleepover with, and to discuss boundaries and shared expectations. Ultimately, you want to be fair and consistent, making sure your response is no different than if your teen were heterosexual. Give your teen opportunities to socialize with their peers in the safety of your home and an opportunity for them to further develop a relationship of mutual trust with you.

What About Dating?

Entering the world of dating is hard for any teen, and can be even harder for your LGBTQ+ child as they try to figure out how to manage the strong romantic emotions and crushes they may be experiencing. Some LGBTQ+ teens feel intimidated about how to approach someone they are attracted to, or don't even know how or where to seek out same-sex dating opportunities. LGBTQ+ teens have the added worry of not knowing what might happen should the object of their affection not be LGBTQ+ or open to a same-sex dating experience. Unfortunately, inadequate and nonexistent same-sex education in many schools has left LGBTQ+ teens having to figure out dating and some of the mechanics of sex on their own.

Talking about LGBTQ+ dating and sex has many parents feeling apprehensive about how to support their teen with experiences they have never had themselves. I cannot emphasize enough how important it is for you to lean into your discomfort and do whatever it takes to help your teen make informed decisions about dating, relationships, and sex. Teens need to learn about STIs, sexual coercion, consent and healthy boundaries, online dating privacy, and safety precautions from possible predators. I encourage parents to also talk about how relationships develop and what makes a good romantic relationship. Acknowledge what you do not know and go online with your teen to find information together. Sharing this experience will allow you to filter credible online sources. By supporting your teen, you will be helping them develop their own confidence and good judgment to make better dating-related decisions.

Encourage Their Passions

As a parent, you can anchor your relationship with your LGBTQ+ teen by supporting them as they seek out and develop their interests and passions. Having interests they feel passionately about helps support your teen's development of a more secure sense of self. I'm guessing you may already have some ideas of your own of what your teen "should" be interested in. Maybe you always imagined them being an athlete or a musician, or loving hiking or reading as much as you do. There's nothing wrong with sharing your ideas, and maybe your teen will consider some of them, but if they don't share your enthusiasm, it will do no good to try to pressure them. It is important to not impose your own opinions, agendas, or judgments, as this will only end up discouraging them. Be honest with yourself about how you might be projecting your own desires and unfulfilled dreams onto your child. Again, the idea is for them to discover their own passions for themself. Allow them to discover their own authentic joy.

FORGIVENESS EXERCISE

You may feel that you haven't done everything perfectly in parenting your LGBTQ+ teen and dealing with their coming out. Perhaps there have been hurtful things said on both sides. These types of regrets can eat away at the foundation of relationships and cause parents to feel discouraged. I am a big believer in the power of forgiveness and compassion as necessary parts of being our best selves and having our most fulfilling relationships.

Take this moment to write your teenager a letter. Don't worry, you don't need to give it to them, though you may choose to do so. This is an exercise meant for you. Take a piece of paper and pen and write by hand a letter to your teen, apologizing for anything you feel you need to make amends for. I want you to really challenge yourself to write honestly and from the heart. Again, this is your process. You will get the most out of this exercise if you do your best to dig deep and speak the truth. I hope when you are done, you will feel more free and able let go of any emotional wounds you have been carrying so that you may show up more fully for yourself and your child.

Give Them (Some) Autonomy

One of the hardest things for a parent to do is to give their teenager space to do things on their own, make their own mistakes, and figure out their authentic self. This can be a scary step because you don't want anything bad to happen to them. It is natural to feel protective of your teen. But gaining autonomy is an important developmental journey so they can find their way to recognizing their strength, their abilities, and their potential. No one likes to feel boxed in or controlled. Teens need to be able to have some freedom in order to figure themselves out.

Many parents do not provide sufficient opportunities for their teens to be independent thinkers and then wonder why their young adult children are having such a hard time figuring out their lives, or why they are not taking personal responsibility for their future. Allowing your teen some autonomy will help nurture and develop the independence skills they will benefit from for the rest of their lives.

Let Teens Be Teens

Easier said than done, I know. But part of parenting an LGBTQ+ teen means supporting them in being who they are—a teenager. Your teen has a lifetime of adulting ahead of them, but these teen years go fast. During this developmental stage of adolescence, parents can sometimes struggle to keep up with their teen's emotional ups and downs, the frequent changes of self-expression, changes in friends and peer groups, feeling excited over an interest or hobby one day and then being over it the next day, and the push and pull between independence and dependence. Though you might be feeling a bit of whiplash, it is very important to try to be patient and just let your teen be a teen. Give them space to be their temperamental, goofy, adventurous, and rambunctious self. At the end of the day, you have to let them be their own person as they experiment and learn how to be in the world.

Remind Them That It Takes Bravery to Be True to Yourself

It is not an easy journey for LGBTQ+ teens to be their authentic selves in a world that can be intolerant or dismissive of difference. Many do not even know yet who or what their true self looks like. Teens and even many adults struggle with that internal voice that brings up feelings of doubt and insecurity: "What will my friends and family think?" "I could never do that," "I am not that smart," "I am ugly," "I'm too weird to fit in anywhere." Intrinsic confidence is created over time and through the affirmations we receive from others and from ourselves, and even then, we are still plagued with self-criticism from time to time.

As a parent, you can facilitate your child's ongoing effort of courage and bravery. One of the most helpful ways you can support your teen is by acknowledging, noticing, and being curious about their shifting interests. This will give them a sense of worth and will help build their confidence to continue their journey of being themself. When you show that you have faith in your teen, you are letting them know it's okay to try new things and it's okay to find out when things don't pan out the way we imagined. All failures are opportunities for learning and growth. Courage does not come from the absence of fear, but from choosing to do something even when we are scared. Every authentic choice your teen makes is a brave step closer to finding out for themself who they are.

Conclusion

This chapter was all about empowering your LGBTQ+ teen to be their authentic self. It can be difficult to manage all the changes and the emotional ups and downs. However, continuing to stand by them and cheering them on through their self-exploration will allow them to develop confidence in themself and thrive as their authentic self. In the next chapter, we will delve into the importance of a supportive network and community to support you and your teen.

"We had people of all backgrounds coming together—all races, all creeds, all colors, all status in life. And coming together, there was a kind of quiet dignity and a kind of sense of caring and a feeling of joint responsibility."

—Dorothy Height

CHAPTER SEVEN

Surround Your Teen with a Supportive Community

This chapter addresses the importance of building a supportive community around your teen and yourself. You have probably heard the saying "It takes a village" to raise a child, and you may already have a community of extended family, friends, teachers, and other parental figures who play large roles in your teen's upbringing and development. The size and details of your supportive community will vary depending on your personal circumstances and where you live. If you do not have anyone currently, I encourage you to invest in finding and creating your own supportive community. You do not have to deal with the challenges you and your LGBTQ+ teen are facing alone. Many feel a sense of shame or embarrassment in asking for help or seeking support. Maybe you feel that this is a private, family matter or you do not want to burden anyone with your problems. I hope by the time you finish reading this chapter, you will feel more open and hopeful about creating a supportive community of resources and people who care about your teen and you.

Casey

Casey is a 16-year-old who identifies as nonbinary and whose pronouns are ze and hir. Casey has never felt like either of the two binary genders, ever since grade school. Ze remembers not being masculine enough to hang out with the boys, and ze was never femme enough to be accepted by the girls at school either. Casey reported struggling with hir self-esteem and hir self-confidence all through middle school and most of high school. Casey luckily had the support of hir mother and father. Casey and hir family live in a small town in the Midwest. Their community is pretty conservative and religious. Over the years, Casey's parents have struggled with adjusting and finding supports within their community, although they do have a few close family friends and extended family who have been their support network. Casey and hir older and younger siblings have had to manage teasing and hurtful interactions because of Casey's gender identity and expression. Casey and hir family have had to educate themselves and continue to find community from LGBTQ+ resources and supports from the nearest metropolitan city, an hour away. When they are unable to make it to the city, they depend on online support groups, communities, and connections who are in similar situations. Casey still struggles to understand hirself and the journey has not been easy. Boundaries have had to be established and reestablished and it feels exhausting, but ze and hir family continue to work through it together with the support of their community.

The Importance of Community

It is from our community that we receive support from others, and it is where we can experience connections and belonging. Our communities come in different shapes and sizes, and these days they are not limited by physical proximity—they can be in the virtual arena, too. For LGBTQ+ teens and their parents, finding and developing a community may not come easily, due to family members who are not accepting, closed-minded churches, or lack of resources, especially for those in smaller or remote communities. However, communities can be found and created if you look for them. There are places for you to find shared values and togetherness, where you can find refuge from others in your life who lack the compassion and the sensitivity you and your teen so desperately need.

When considering your community, start by thinking about what you need and what you are looking for. Are you looking for the support of other parents of LGBTQ+ teens? Are you looking for a space to get involved to promote LGBTQ+ issues? Are you looking for resources to help your teen? Allow your individual needs and interests to lead you to explore your community. Even if one does not exist, trust you are not alone in your need, and it may be possible for you to start your own community you find lacking.

Tips for Building a
Support System

With a little bit of time and effort, it can be easier than you think to create a support system. Here are a few tips on how you can build the team you need.

Look for local resources – Explore LGBTQ+ agencies and groups already established in your community or nearby communities.

Ask for help – Find support in places of worship that are LGBTQ+ affirming, your local library, chamber of commerce, LGBTQ+-sponsored events (Pride events), PFLAG, mental health professionals, the Trevor Project, HRC (Human Rights Campaign), and GLSEN (Gay, Lesbian & Straight Education Network).

Get involved – Seek out clubs, local health centers, medical groups, religious groups who are LGBTQ+ allies, activist groups, and other ways you can make a difference.

Friends and family – Reach out to family and friends who you already know are LGBTQ+ supportive.

Virtual supports – Even if you are in a small community, as long as you have a computer or a smartphone, you can search and connect with a wide range of virtual support groups and resources for LGBTQ+ teens and their families.

A SOLID SUPPORT SYSTEM

We all need people and resources we can depend on. A solid support system will provide you with the support and information to best navigate through the newness of the LGBTQ+ world. It will influence positive growth and learning; nurture a sense of belonging through connection; and potentially mitigate your teen's feelings of isolation, depression, and anxiety, lessening risks of substance use and abuse. A solid support system will calm your sense of fear and instead strengthen your confidence, as you know there are others who are going through it, too. The more you can surround yourself with affirming support systems, the more you will be able to develop a supportive and compassionate environment for your teen.

LEARN FROM PEOPLE WHO ARE DIFFERENT

There is a huge LGBTQ+ world out there with a lot of knowledge, love, and compassion. So go with an open mind and heart, and explore for yourself who and what is out there, and you will find the support you are seeking for yourself and your LGBTQ+ teen. The LGBTQ+ community of teens and parents come from all walks of life and different cultures, beliefs, and values. Learn from their experiences and stories.

YOU CAN'T GIVE YOUR TEEN EVERYTHING THEY NEED ALL THE TIME

As much as you love and want to support your LGBTQ+ teen, it is important for you to recognize you cannot do it all. It is not realistic, nor is it a fair expectation to have of yourself. You may be doing a disservice to your child by trying to do everything yourself, when there are other people, including professionals, who might be able to offer specific help with your unique needs. You and your teen will be going through changes along the way, so it is important to also realize your team will grow and evolve as your needs change over time.

▌ SAFETY PLAN

One of the best ways to support yourself and your teen is by having a safety or crisis plan. Many times, we become paralyzed in a crisis, unable to think clearly and respond in a skillful way. Being proactive and creating a plan can minimize panic and offer comfort. Here is framework you can use for you and your LGBTQ+ teen. Ideally, this is something you can create together, allowing your teen to feel involved and empowered in the creation process rather than having it dictated to them. If your teen is part of the creation of plans and rules, there is buy-in from the start.

1. Get a piece of paper and pen or type up a table like the one shown here.

2. Think about the different uncomfortable or stressful situations you or your teen might find yourselves in.

3. Identify ways each situation can be dealt with.

4. Post the plan somewhere it will be easily accessible when needed

SITUATION	WHAT I CAN DO . . .
I feel like hurting myself.	• Reach out to my parents. • Call a friend. • Call the Suicide Prevention Lifeline (800-273-8255).
I feel lonely.	• Call a friend. • Listen to music that makes me happy. • Watch my favorite TV show. • Reach out to my parents. • Go rollerblading.
I got threatened or bullied at school.	• Tell a trusted teacher. • Ask a friend to help. • Speak to my counselor. • Talk to the principal.
I am feeling overwhelmed.	• Take a walk. • Talk to my parents. • Go do something fun. • Go work out. • Draw. • Journal.
I have a problem and I don't know how to fix it.	• Ask for help. • Talk to a friend or parents for advice. • Ask my online support group for ideas. • Speak to my counselor.

Your LGBTQ+ Teen Will Face Prejudice

Let's face it. Your LGBTQ+ teen will continue to face various degrees of homophobia, internalized homophobia, transphobia, biphobia, and other kinds of LGBTQ+ fears and prejudices for the rest of their life. There have been huge cultural improvements in tolerance and inclusion, but in recent years, there has also been a lot of regression of safety measures and legal protections that were previously in place. Prejudice comes in different forms— bias, microaggressions, social exclusion, bigotry, hate speech and acts, discrimination, and political oppression. It can come from expected places such as conservative politicians and bigoted family members, as well as from the individuals and institutions you least expect: your church, school, work, family, friends, cultural community, social groups—the list goes on. You can buffer the painful judgments and voices by making sure you surround yourself with supports to help you get through adversarial situations and people.

How can you and your LGBTQ+ teen deal with prejudice? One of the most empowering ways is to for you to get involved in your community as an ally. Find a local group or organization that advocates and actively works against LGBTQ+ prejudice. If the prejudice is occurring in your child's school or at your church, then you can stand up there to advocate for your teen. If your teen wants to advocate for themselves, you can stand by them and encourage them. At the very least, listening and asking your teen how you can help will be validating and encouraging. As a parent, providing a loving and stable foundation and doing the work of instilling a strong sense of self and resilience in your teen will help them navigate the challenges they will face throughout their life.

You Set the Tone for How Your Community Treats Your Child

The way others respond and treat your LGBTQ+ teen is largely established by you. Your family, your other children, your spouse, neighbors, friends, and your teen's teachers and coaches will all be looking to you, taking note of your politics, watching how you interact with your teen, and listening to how you speak to, and about, your child and other LGBTQ+ people. People in your life and your child's life may initially respond in their own way, but you have the voice and the power to protect your teen from your community when it is needed.

Teaching others how to treat your teen is your responsibility, whether you like it or not. You may not be acutely aware of it, but you influence the standards and the expectations of others. For example, how do you react if you hear others speaking negatively, even under the guise of humor, about LGBTQ+ people? Do you just keep quiet? Or do you let them know you have a teen who is LGBTQ+ and their jokes or comments are unappreciated? What about if your child's school dismisses creating a safe space for your teen? Advocating and sticking up for your teen not only helps create a safe and supportive community, it also shows your child you have their back. By standing up for them, you are modeling how they can stand up for themself and be treated with respect.

The following conversation illustrates how a parent and their LGBTQ+ teenager can talk about the value of having a support network and what that might look like. James, a 14-year-old, cisgender, gay teen is having problems with feeling depressed and unmotivated lately. James's parent is concerned about what to do.

Parent: James, I just want to check in on how you have been feeling lately. I know you said you are still feeling sad often.

James: Yeah, Mom, I really don't know what is going on with me. Things are better at school, but I still don't feel right.

Parent: Well, I have tried to encourage you to talk your school counselor, hang out with your friends, and just get out more. Maybe it's time we go about this differently. What do you think? What else or who else do you think could help?

James: I know I told you I didn't want to do a support group or take medications, but maybe it's time.

Parent: Okay, so let's talk to your counselor about adding a psychiatrist to your support team. We can also check out what might be available through the LGBTQ+ center in the city, or online. If you have the time now, let's go online together and see what's out there.

James: Okay, sure, I really appreciate your help. I don't think I could do this alone. My friends are great but they aren't always available and don't always know how to help.

Parent: Everyone helps in different ways. This is why we need some other supports in place, too. So you have some other options.

Set Guidelines for Friends and Family

Even within our own friends and family members, it is sometimes necessary to set guidelines or expectations for how they should treat your LGBTQ+ teen. It is important to let friends and family know your teen deserves to be treated kindly and with respect, even if they may have their own opinions or beliefs about LGBTQ+ people. For example, you may have to remind people repeatedly about your transgender child's new name and pronouns. Your responsibility to your teen is to protect them and to support them through maintaining a loving and accepting support network. Surround yourself with family and friends who help raise you up instead of tearing your down. I know this is not easy, and I also recognize this might involve decisions and actions you would rather not have to deal with, such as having difficult conversations with extended family or letting go of some friends. With immediate family, it can be trickier and will require more finesse setting expectations and guidelines since you all live under the same roof.

NUCLEAR FAMILY

If your LGBTQ+ teen has come out to you alone, it is important to include regular conversations with them about how they would like to come out to the rest of the family, and if they are already out, ask them what specific challenges they are encountering. I encourage you and the rest of your nuclear family to take whatever time is needed and keep the conversations between everyone open and accessible. Establish some rules to keep conversations respectful as family members ask questions and talk about how the family is changing. As things come up, don't let them fester or get shoved under the rug. Address things and deal with the growing pains you are all experiencing as they come up.

YOUR OTHER CHILDREN

Having a LGBTQ+ sibling come out can be confusing to your other kids. The different ages and the reactions of your other children will determine how you need to respond and support the needs of all your kids. In cases where there is name, gender identity, or gender expression change, it is even more important to provide clarity and guidance in the most sensitive and compassionate way. Encourage your other children to still be kind and loving of their LGBTQ+ sibling, even if they do not completely understand.

EXTENDED FAMILY

Extended family can be valuable part of your supportive community, but the truth is they can also be a mixed bag. Expect there will be some family members who simply cannot be a support, and that will have to be okay. Focus on those family members who are accepting and validating. Do your best to ask them to respect the name or pronouns that your LGBTQ+ teen identifies with. Take every opportunity to set firm boundaries, and also be patient with their adjustment as well.

FRIENDS

The most significant members of your teen's support network are their friends, and you can support these relationships by extending a warm and inviting attitude toward your child's social circle. These friends should validate them, stand up for them, and accept them for who they are and how they are changing. Teach your teen that having "cool" or popular friends is not really important; what matters most is surrounding themself with friends who help them feel good about being themself and provide safety from an environment that can sometimes be rejecting. If you know of certain friends who are not supportive, you could encourage your teen to rethink those friendships. In situations causing harm, you can set a firm boundary about who you will and will not allow in your home.

TEACHERS

It may be necessary for you to assess your teen's learning environment and facilitate ways that help your teen feel safe to fully learn and succeed academically. Teachers can be added eyes and ears so that you can better understand and support your teen. Help your teen identify one or two teachers whom they can speak to when they are having a hard day, or go to for help dealing with challenges at school. Likewise, if you know of a teacher who is failing at creating a safe learning environment for your child, such as allowing teasing or bullying, or even participating in it, it is your responsibility to advocate for your teen and speak to someone who can correct the problem.

Professional Counselors/Therapists Can Also Be Part of Your Community

There might come a point when either you and your teen might want to include a professional counselor or a mental health therapist as part of your support community. A therapist can provide either one of you with a safe, neutral, and private space to talk about challenges you are facing. Sometimes there are emotions, thoughts, and other relationship challenges you may not feel comfortable talking about with your spouse and close friends. Likewise, your LGBTQ+ teen may have topics they do not feel comfortable talking to you about, even though you have made every attempt to be inviting. Counselors and mental health therapists can provide you with support around challenging developmental as well as emotional challenges, such as feelings of depression, anxiety, trauma, and gender identity and expression. When searching for a counselor or therapist for you or your child, make sure to ask if they are LGBTQ+ inclusive and have experience in this area.

Don't Give In to Social Pressure

Lots of people have an opinion on how you should parent your LGBTQ+ teen. You might be feeling confused and unsure, so you have been soliciting the advice and guidance of your closest friends and family. The problem with the advice of others, as well-intentioned as they may be, is that they cannot possibly know every detail of whatever challenges you are facing. They are not living your life, and their advice is based only on what you tell them and whatever preconceived notions or baggage they bring with them. Maybe you live in a conservative community, ignorant of LGBTQ+ issues. I don't think I have to tell you how harmful this would be for your LGBTQ+ teen. You may indeed find wisdom and support from a variety of outside sources, but at the end of the day, it is your life, your teen, and your family you are dealing with, and I want to empower you to trust in yourself and your decisions. You know—and love—your LGBTQ+ teen better than anyone else.

Don't Be Afraid to Set Hard Boundaries When Someone Crosses a Line

It can be quite difficult and painful when someone has crossed a line with you and your LGBTQ+ teen, and it may require you to have hard conversations and make difficult decisions. Maybe you have a brother-in-law who will not stop teasing your gay son for his feminine gender expression. Maybe your mother refuses to call your transgender daughter by her new name and correct pronouns. By letting these microaggressions continue, you are sending your teen the message you do not have their back and will not stand up for them when they are being harmed. It is imperative that you set a hard boundary against threats or disrespectful actions from others. Saying things such as "You're overreacting" or "It was just a joke" minimizes and gaslights your teen's painful experience and will result in a loss of trust.

It is also possible your teen doesn't know what their own boundaries are or can't recognize when they're being crossed. Having conversations about boundaries is essential. Help your teen understand why boundaries are important and what they represent in terms of your child's protection and overall well-being. When your teen's boundaries have been crossed and they do not know how to stand up for themself, this is when you need to step in and talk to them about your concerns. Again, you are your teen's protector and role model. Helping your teen learn at an early age how to set clear boundaries with others, and how to access support when they cannot do it alone, will give your teen permission to ask for help when they need it.

Seek Out Role Models for Your Child

One of the ways you can help your teen create a supportive community is by helping them find role models. You can start by talking with your teen and helping them identify what values, strengths, and skills appeal to them. Role models don't have to be famous or historical figures. They are all around you and your teen; it is just a matter of being able to recognize them. A role model could be a next-door neighbor who always has a smile on her face and says hi whenever she sees you and your family. They could be an out LGBTQ+ musical artist whose songs are empowering and hopeful. They could be a trailblazing activist who is working hard to defend the rights of kids like yours.

Role models give your teen someone to look up to and admire, which can help their own goals and dreams as they evolve into their LGBTQ+ self. Your teen's journey of understanding and self-discovery can be fueled by individuals who have overcome the challenges that your teen is currently facing and who represent hope for who your teen might want to become. Encourage your teen to think about their dreams and values, and then support them in finding someone who symbolizes them.

LET THEM CHOOSE THEIR OWN ROLE MODELS

Teens want to have role models they can relate to and look up to, and who inspire them to reach for their unique, individual dreams. As your teen evolves, the role models they identify with will also change. Focus on the positive influences of their chosen role models, and trust that your LGBTQ+ teen knows best who and what gives them hope.

Seek Out Role Models for Yourself

Similarly, you also need role models who can help guide and support you through your personal journey and who can normalize your struggles and feelings. Role models can provide you with a sense of hope when you are feeling lost and confused. They could be a fellow parent who is dealing with the same issues you are facing, someone who exemplifies compassion and healthy communication with their child, someone you can relate to culturally, or someone who is of the same religion. The idea is to find individuals who inspire you and provide you with a hopeful vision of what you would like for yourself.

Don't Be Afraid to Ask for Help

Many of us have been taught that asking for help or relying on others makes us appear weak or imposes our burdens on other people. Socially, we stress independence and self-sufficiency. I am here to tell you that message is completely incorrect and potentially harmful. It's important to recognize times when we simply do not have all the answers and need to ask for help. No parent ever feels as if they have everything figured out, and having the expectation that you should only leads to disappointment and feelings of inadequacy. Asking for help is brave.

Embrace getting comfortable with being vulnerable with others. I encourage you to let go of the do-it-all-by-yourself model. Give yourself the opportunity to learn from the wisdom and experiences of others. You will be a better parent, and both you and your teen will benefit.

When to Ask for Help

There will be times when you and/or your LGBTQ+ teen will need some additional help. The following are some signs that should prompt you to seek out help.

Overwhelm – You have reached a point where you are at a loss and do not know what else to do. You have tried to find answers and direction, but you are at your wit's end. With all that you have going on in your life, you simply cannot do it alone. Seek personal or professional support.

Suicidal thoughts and self-harming behaviors – If your teen has shared thoughts and feelings of wanting to hurt themself or is actively self-harming, such as cutting, then it is time to get professional help for your teen.

School troubles – If your teen is having trouble at school (bullying, academics, teachers), then it's time to intervene and get support to stabilize the situation.

Drugs and substance use/abuse – Sometimes your teen is dealing with so much, they turn to drugs and alcohol for an escape or to numb the pain. If experimentation seems to have gotten out of control, get professional support to mitigate ongoing use and abuse.

At-risk sexual behaviors – Difficulties with excessive pornography or unsafe sexual activity could be an indication that help is needed to support safer and less risky sexual habits.

It Takes a Village

It truly does take a village. A village made up of friends, family, school leaders, church leaders, community leaders, and many other LGBTQ+-affirming partners. The challenges you and your teen will face through this journey can be managed with the help of others. You do not have to figure it all out on your own. But you must be willing to open yourself up and seek out the help you need. I get that it can feel a bit vulnerable to open up your family life to others, but in doing so, you will find you are not alone in this journey. You do not have to feel shame because you are struggling with how to care for yourself and your LGBTQ+ teen. There are so many incredibly knowledgeable and caring individuals and agencies who want to assist parents just like you and teens just like your teen. Give yourself permission and comfort to learn and heal with the help of others.

Conclusion

Having a support network comprised of a broad range of key figures will be a tremendous support to you and your LGBTQ+ teen. This can be challenging for those who live in rural communities or communities where there may be less than warm attitudes and beliefs about LGBTQ+ individuals. Thankfully, through the internet, isolated teens and their families can access resources they would otherwise not have available to them. You do not have to struggle on your own. There are people out there—some you already know, some you will need to seek out—who care and are willing to help make your adjustment and moments of difficulty a little bit easier. You can create the support network that best suits you, your teen, and your family.

■ ■ ■ ■ ■ ■ ■ ■ ■ ■

"Teamwork begins by building trust. And the only way to do that is to overcome our need for invulnerability."

—*Patrick Lencioni*

PART III

What to Do When . . .

In this section, I am going to share some frequently asked questions and answers covering a broad range of common scenarios faced by parents of LGBTQ+ teens. These are questions I have been asked in my therapy room over the years, and they address a variety of topics such as boundary setting, supporting a teen's emotional needs, and managing a lack of LGBTQ+ support at school. I have tried very hard to share a range of situations; however, this is by no means a complete account of all the unique questions and situations every family will face. But I do hope you will be able to find some glimmer of solace, hope, and helpful ideas from others' experiences. Know that many other parents have also dealt with some of the same challenges you are now facing.

q I have five children and one of them is lesbian. Should I be worried about my other children being gay or lesbian, too?

a Just because you already have one lesbian child does not mean your other children will necessarily turn out to be LGBTQ+ also. It certainly is not unusual for there to be more than one LGBTQ+ child in the family, but having one LGBTQ+ child is by no means a predictor.

What I would suggest you think about is what it would mean to you if you had more than one LGBTQ+ child. It could be beneficial for you to think about what you have learned already and how you might respond differently if you were confronted with another child who is somewhere on the LGBTQ+ spectrum. You might consider talking to your lesbian teen and asking them how your reaction and support could have been better.

q It has been over a year now since my teenage son came out as bisexual. I keep waiting for him to decide if he is gay or not. I asked him a few times when he first came out, but we just ended up getting into an argument. I don't want to pressure him by asking him about it anymore. What should I do?

a I first want to say exploring one's sexual orientation and experimenting with different sexual ideas and experiences is a normal part of adolescence, and it's often necessary in the process of gaining clarity about one's identity. Teenagers these days are also much more open and fluid with their sexuality. But let's assume your son already feels clear about his sexual orientation. He currently identifies as bisexual, and I encourage you to work on being able to accept and support him as he is, to allow your son the space to accept himself, and to give him the confirmation that you love him no matter whom he chooses to physically, emotionally, or relationally be with. Some examples of supportive things you can say are "I'd really like to hear how you feel" and "Can you tell me what it's been like for you?"

q **My teenage daughter came home from school the other day very upset. All she does is hide out in her room, and she hasn't seemed like herself for a while. I asked her what was wrong, and she told me she has a crush on one of her female friends, who also happens to go to our church. She has been conflicted and wonders if this means she's a lesbian. I didn't know how to respond to her. How do I help her?**

a Just because your teenage daughter has a crush on another girl does not automatically mean she is a lesbian (or bisexual or pansexual). It also does not mean that she isn't. It is not uncommon for someone to crush on someone of the same gender identity during their lifetime. Sexuality is fluid and not set in stone, and attraction to others is not always sexual. I would suggest you first find a way to let your daughter know you are available to support, listen, and love her no matter what. Assure her she doesn't need to figure it all out right now. Ask her how you can be of support to her. She might not feel completely comfortable talking to you, and if this is the case, ask if there is someone else she would be more comfortable talking with, such as another family member, a teacher, or someone at your church, assuming your church is open to LGBTQ+ individuals.

q **My son came out as transgender recently and we've been pretty lax with our family rules so as not to push him away. Now he is refusing to comply with any of our expectations around social media use. How do I create boundaries that work for all of us?**

a For many parents, regardless of their child's sexual orientation and gender identity, it can be a challenge to balance

being sensitive and supportive while also providing structure and setting clear boundaries. Both are very important
aspects of creating a healthy parent and teen relationship.
In this situation, I would first sit down with your teen and
express to them what you have been noticing about their
behaviors and how you are feeling about it. Be sure there is
no room for your teen to think your reaction has anything to
do with them being transgender. It's also important for you
to acknowledge you understand social media is a big part
of teenage life, but you are concerned that the amount of
time spent on social media is taking away from family time,
or that you have noticed their grades are suffering. Let them
know changes need to happen and you would like to hear
from them what they think balance can look like. You could
also ask them about their own ideas about consequences if
social media time continues to be a hindrance to their overall
success and well-being.

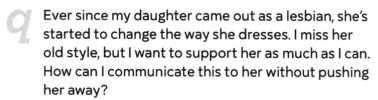

**Ever since my daughter came out as a lesbian, she's
started to change the way she dresses. I miss her
old style, but I want to support her as much as I can.
How can I communicate this to her without pushing
her away?**

You know that old saying "If you can't say anything nice, then
don't say anything at all"? I think it very much applies in this
specific situation. I would suggest you talk to a close friend,
family member, or support group about your feelings and
opinions in order to vent and find validation. It may also be
helpful for you to dig deep and try to understand why it is
so important to you how your daughter dresses. If you really
find yourself needing to communicate how you feel, then try
to find a softer and more supportive way to talk to her. An
example might be something like "I want for us to have an
open and safe space to communicate with each other, but I
worry about hurting your feelings. It's just sometimes I miss

how you used to dress and your style. It's important to me that you know I am trying. Please know I love you, and I want you to dress in whatever way makes you feel strong and confident."

Teens will often experiment with how they dress and how they want to express themselves with hair, makeup, and the clothing and accessories they wear. Allow your teen to figure out what dress and style feeds their strength, bravery, and authentic expression of themself.

q **My teen has made it clear we should refer to him using proper pronouns. My father (their grandfather) straight up refuses and makes a big deal about it every time we are together. Family dinners and celebrations have gotten so tense my child now refuses to attend. What can I do? How do I keep the peace?**

a In this situation you have two people whom you care about, and you want to be able to keep both of them happy. It may take some time for your father, because of generational differences and attitudes, to adjust. Old habits die hard. However, you should not force your teen to continue to put themself in hurtful situations, even with family. My suggestion is to sit down with your father and help him better understand how his behavior is affecting you and your teen. Let him know how hurtful it is whenever he does not refer to your teen by their new name and correct pronouns, as has been requested of him repeatedly. Acknowledge you know it is hard, and maybe share how this transition has been a struggle for you, too. Your teen needs to have your support and you need to stand up for them. If things are really bad, then it might be time to set some boundaries and limits. For example, telling your father if he cannot at least try to get better at referencing your teen properly and respectfully, then there might need to be some changes to your participation in family dinners and celebrations.

q My teenage son is gay and is asking to have a sleepover with his boyfriend. I don't know how comfortable I am with his request. What should I do?

a I can certainly understand how this would be a tough decision to make. As a parent, I would start by exploring what your specific concerns are. Do you worry they will be having sex under your roof? Are you worried about the boyfriend's parents being upset with you for not setting more boundaries, or afraid other parents will judge you and think you are a bad parent? Is it an issue about trust? Do you feel uncomfortable with same-sex displays of affection? Get clarity for yourself about what is at the root of your feelings and thoughts.

I think you also have to consider the tolerance and acceptance level of your family as a whole. If you have another parental figure in the household, what are their feelings about it? You should set rules that are fair and respectful to both of you and the rest of the family. Then I would sit down with your son and talk about your thoughts and feelings about his request. If you are not yet ready, then let your son know this, and that you need a little bit more time to get comfortable with the idea. Ideally, you want to give him a time frame so he isn't left worrying for an unknown amount of time. For example, "Let me get back to you on this in a couple weeks."

q *a* Did I cause my teen to be LGBTQ+?

This is a question I get often. The simple answer is no. A person's sexual orientation and gender identity is believed to be more about genetics, and every person's experience is different for how they gain awareness of their orientation and identity. Your question would suggest you feel a level of responsibility or fault for your teen's sexual orientation and or gender identity. Your teen is LGBTQ+ for similar reasons that they might have a natural ability at playing a sport, be naturally artistic, be a certain height, or have a certain hair color. It's just how they were made. I encourage you to focus more on supporting and loving your teen for who they are, rather than worrying about the cause. You can quell your angst and deepen your understanding by talking to your teen about their experience and listening to them share about how they have come to understand themself. The more you learn, the more you will feel assured this is not because of anything you have done.

 My wife and I have a 13-year-old daughter who came out six months ago and identified herself as a cisgender lesbian. I have tried really hard to be there for her, and I think in some ways we have gotten closer. But my wife and my daughter are still having problems and I feel caught in the middle. How do I get my wife and my daughter to get along better?

 The reality is your relationship and your wife's relationship with your daughter are two separate journeys. As much as you want them both to get along, it is not your responsibility to repair their relationship. I think it would be helpful for you to talk with your wife and your daughter individually and let each of them know how you feel about them not getting along. Ask them if there is anything you can do to help. It may be you simply need to be patient with both of them and give them each time to figure out their relationship with one another. It might be helpful to suggest they seek professional support to help them communicate and work through their issues so you do not have to be caught in the middle.

q What does it mean when my teen uses the terms *nonbinary, gender nonconforming,* and *genderqueer*? I often get them confused and cannot keep them straight.

a I want to first acknowledge all the different terminology is confusing to many people, sometimes even for those on the LGBTQ+ spectrum. So don't beat yourself up over being confused. The term *nonbinary* refers to someone's gender identity, how they see themself (male, female, somewhere in between, or outside those identities altogether), and how they want to express their identity. *Gender nonconforming* has nothing to do with one's identity but is simply about expression. Regardless of sexual orientation, a gender-nonconforming person does not subscribe exclusively to rigid societal expectations of either masculinity or femininity. A heterosexual cisgender boy can express themself in gender nonconforming ways, such as wearing girl's cloths, having longer hair, wearing makeup, or wearing nail polish. At the same time, a gender nonconforming lesbian can choose to express herself by having shorter hair, preferring to wear neutral clothing like T-shirts and jeans, and also wearing makeup. *Genderqueer* is similar to and often used interchangeably with *nonbinary*. *Genderqueer* can also be about one's presentation, in the same way as *gender noncomforming*. Genderqueer individuals embrace a sense of fluidity and feel less restrictiveness in their identification, with some allowing changes from time to time. Some identities that can fall into this term are *agender, pangender,* and *demigender,* though genderqueer is the most commonly used identifier.

q How do I know what supports my transgender teen's needs?

a As with any LGBTQ+ teen, a good place to start is to let them know you love and care for them, and then ask them directly how you can be of support. Being transgender is uniquely difficult compared to other experiences along the LGBTQ+ spectrum, with its own set of evolutions and degrees of needs. Your teen might want to seek out HRT (hormone replacement therapy), which means taking hormones to make temporary as well as permanent physiological changes, or gender affirming surgery. Some might want to simply alter their outward appearance by the way they dress and style their hair, or they may use chest binders. There are some who might decide they do not want to do anything at all at this time. The most important thing is to consider to what degree your teen will feel comfortable not only in their body, but also in your community. Meet your child where they are and let them know you will stand by them through it all. In addition, there are other supports such as mental health professionals, medical professionals, online and local transgender communities, and other supportive resources.

 I love my teen and I want to be supportive, but I just feel sad all the time and I cannot stop crying. When will I start to feel better?

 Unfortunately I cannot tell you when you will start to feel better. I simply do not know.

But what I will say is to be patient with yourself and your teen. Your teen has more than likely had a lot of time to think about how and when they would come out to you, but this is all relatively new to you, and it will take some time to get used to. Allow yourself time to understand and accept your teen's coming out. The reason it is difficult is because it may have been an unexpected shock, or maybe you have always had suspicions but hoped you would be proven wrong. The most important thing is to take care of your LGBTQ+ teen and to take care of yourself and your immediate family. Try your best to minimize crying in front of your teen, as they could develop a sense of guilt and resentment around perceiving their identity to be the cause. I encourage you to talk to people you trust and feel comfortable with. You do not have to go through this alone. If you don't have any close friends or family, then are there many mental health professionals you can talk to. Seek out LGBTQ+ groups, either in your community or online. Continue to keep the lines of communication open with your teen. Ask them questions and listen to them. In time, you will find that things will get easier.

 My teen came out to me about two years ago. It has been rough, but we are managing as best we can. I am concerned because my teen has been irritable, spends a lot of time away from the family, and has been refusing to go to school sometimes. What should I do?

 There could be a lot of different things going on with your teen that can explain their behaviors. However, you won't truly know unless you ask them. It is not unusual for LGBTQ+ teens to experience hardships that cause them to develop or fuel an underlying mental health disorder. They may be experiencing social and emotional adversity due to bullying, prejudice, lack of support, rejection, substance use, and other types of physical or sexual trauma. If they are turning those challenges inward, life may feel even more difficult. I would suggest you talk to your teen and let them know you have been noticing them behaving a certain way and you want to make sure they are okay. Remind them you are there to help them and support them through whatever might be going on. From there you can figure out how to help. Don't be hurt if your teen doesn't want to disclose or talk about what they are dealing with and prefers to talk to someone else, like a mental health professional.

q I have a 16-year-old son and I have always wondered if he might be gay. He has female friends who often come to our home, but he has never expressed an interest in dating. Should I just ask him?

a Coming out is a personal decision. If your teen is indeed gay and has not yet come out to you, it probably means that he is not ready. I encourage parents in these types of situations to simply let their child know they are available to talk and to make sure their child knows they are open to LGBTQ+ people. There are different ways you can let your teen know you would support and love them if they are LGBTQ+ without explicitly putting them on the spot. When parents show interest and approval of LGBTQ+-themed TV shows and other media, out celebrities, people in the community, as well as political support for LGBTQ+ causes, they communicate to their kids that they are open and validating. Coming out can be difficult for teens, and for anyone at any age for that matter. As long as you have a strong and safe connection, you can trust they will come out to you and share with you when they are ready.

q I have a transgender teen who attends a local high school. My teen has been out at school and continues to be a victim of ongoing bullying and teasing. I have spoken to the school already, and they just seem to not care. How do I support my teen so they can be safe at school?

a This is a challenge for many LGBTQ+ students. Unfortunately, depending on where you live, your school district, and your community's values and beliefs, the degree of affirming and protective measures in schools will vary quite a bit. However, your teen's school has an ethical obligation to protect and allow for a safe learning environment for all students. If you have already dealt with the school and feel you are not getting the degree of support you need, I would suggest writing a letter documenting your concerns and the supportive response you are asking for in support of your LGBTQ+ teen. You can also reach out to the superintendent of your school district. LGBTQ+ organizations such as PFLAG and GLSEN can offer support. You can also speak to your teen's individual teachers, at least those who you know are LGBTQ+ allies. If there is a GSA (Gay Straight Alliance), encourage your teen to get involved. Overall, I encourage you to seek out further help and know that you do not have to take on this endeavor alone.

A Final Note

From the bottom of my heart, I genuinely hope this book has given you some much-needed guidance, information, and encouragement to be a brighter light of hope for your LGBTQ+ teen—and for yourself. Feel reassured the effort you put forth in educating yourself about LGBTQ+ challenges and needs means a tremendous amount to your teen. I want to thank you for loving your teen even though you might not have all the answers, nor fully understand them just yet. By seeking out the resources and support offered in this book, you have stepped up and affirmed your love and support of your child.

I wrote this book because there are still so many parents out there who feel lost, confused, and hurting. In chapter 1, I wanted to honor and acknowledge the fact many parents have a challenging time transitioning from being a parent of a young child to being a parent of a teenager, and being a parent of an LGBTQ+ teen presents its own unique challenges. The more you understand these challenges, the better you can be at making the necessary adjustments that will define how you connect with and support your child, and how you grow and improve as a parent. In chapter 2, we shifted to deepening your knowledge about issues affecting LGBTQ+ teens. Having an awareness of the situations your teen might be facing will help you keep a pulse on what your teen may need your support in figuring out. In chapters 3 and 4, we focused on how you can establish a strong foundation for your teen and how to have the tough but necessary conversations. Part of what will help you successfully work as a team with your teen is having a solid platform to launch from, and that starts by taking an honest look at yourself. Being able to have honest conversations that target sensitive topics and push you both out of your comfort zones will help create a sense of security, trust, and shared confidence. Chapters 5 and 6 focused on rebuilding and cementing your relationship in a new and improved way. As you continue to accept your new and ever-changing relationship with your teen, you will be helping them also discover their own inner strength as they endeavor to develop their authentic self. Chapter 7 highlighted the value of finding and developing your own support network so that you do not have to walk this path alone.

I wish you, your family, and your LGBTQ+ teen courage, curiosity, hope, and patience as you embark on this incredible path of self-discovery, healing, and ultimately, peace. The journey will demand a lot of you, but the payoff will be well worth it. Trust that by using the information and tools I have provided you in this book, you will find confidence and success as a parent and strengthen the connection you have with your LGBTQ+ teen.

Best of luck to you,
Allan

Glossary

ally: an individual who supports and advocates for the rights of LGBTQ+ individuals and the community at large

aromantic or **aro:** an individual who experiences little or no romantic attraction to others and might also have no desire to form a romantic relationship

asexual or **ace:** an individual who has little or no sexual attraction and might also not experience sexual desire

binding: when one's chest is constricted for the purposes of reducing the appearance of having breasts

bisexual: when a person is attracted to those of the same gender and also those of other gender identities

butch: when a person's gender expression is masculine

cisgender: an individual whose gender identity matches the sex they were assigned at birth

cross-dressing: when an individual wears the clothing of the "opposite" binary sex or gender identity

demisexual: a person who needs to develop an emotional connection in order to have a sexual relationship

femme: when a person's gender expression is feminine

gay: an individual who is emotionally, romantically, or sexually attracted to someone who identifies as the same gender; this identifier can be used by men and women

gender-affirming surgery (GAS): a range of surgical options that affirm a sense of congruence between one's outward body and their inner self; these can include genital surgery, as well as chest surgery and facial treatments

gender binary: the idea that male and female are the only two genders, and that all people must identify with only one of them

gender expression: how an individual expresses their gender identity by the way they dress and behave to the outside world

genderfluid: when a person does not identify as one set gender identity and might shift between different identities

gender identity: one's internal sense of self as male, female, both, neither, or somewhere else on the gender spectrum

gender nonconforming or **GNC:** when someone expresses themself outside the confines of masculine and feminine societal norms

genderqueer: an individual whose gender identity or gender expression is outside of the rigid male and female binary

intersex: when an individual's birth anatomy is not clearly consistent as male or female; they are born with variations of differences with their sex traits and reproductive anatomy

lesbian: a woman or woman-aligned nonbinary person who is sexually and romantically oriented toward the same gender

outing: this is when an individual's sexual orientation, gender identity, or gender expression is shared without their consent

nonbinary: an individual who does not identify as exclusively male or exclusively female

pansexual: an individual who can be emotionally and romantically attracted to others of any gender identity

Pride: an annual worldwide celebration of the LGBTQ+ identities

queer: an individual who identifies with an orientation outside of heterosexuality and/or an identity outside cisgender and/or an intersex identity

questioning: a period when a person is experimenting or curious about exploring their sexual orientation, gender identity, and/or gender expression

sexual orientation: an individual's emotional, romantic, and physical attraction to another person

transgender: an individual whose gender identity does not match the sex they were assigned at birth

transition: the social, legal, and medical steps a transgender person might take in order to live more openly as their gender identity

Two-Spirit: Indigenous people who identify with both a male and a female spirit

Resources

Books

Beyond Magenta: Transgender Teens Speak Out, by Susan Kuklin: Stories of six real-life transgender teens that can offer you a broad understanding of what it means to be transgender.

The Gender Creative Child: Pathways for Nurturing and Supporting Children Who Live Outside Gender Boxes, by Diane Ehrensaft: An excellent resource about gender identity and expression.

The Savvy Ally: A Guide for Becoming a Skilled LGBTQ+ Advocate, by Jeannie Gainsburg: Learn about how to be more supportive of LGBTQ+ individuals.

This Book Is Gay, by Juno Dawson: An easy way to learn more and read with your teen.

Podcasts

Gender Reveal: Deals with trans, nonbinary, and Two-Spirit experiences.

LGBTQ&A: Learn from global LGBTIA+ public figures.

Outspoken Voices: Perspectives of LGBTQ+ people and their LGBTQ+ family members.

Queery: Focuses on guests who can speak to the LGBTQ+ experience.

Rated LGBTO+ Radio: Addresses a variety of LGBTQ+ topics.

Support Services

LGBTQ+ National Help Center (1-888-843-4564): free LGBTQ+ support and local resources

National Suicide Prevention Lifeline (1-800-273-8255): 24/7 crisis line

The Trevor Project (1-866-488-7386): supportive hotline for LGBTQ+ teens

Websites

Human Rights Campaign (HRC.org): the largest LGBTQ+ advocacy organization

Impact: The LGBTQ+ Health and Development Program (ImpactProgram.org): informative resource supporting a broad range of LGBTQ+ issues

PFLAG (PFLAG.org): an invaluable resource for parents and LGBTQ+ community

The Trevor Project (TheTrevorProject.org): excellent resource for LGBTQ+ teens

Trans Lifeline (TransLifeline.org): a resource for helping you get community transgender support

Trans Youth Equality Foundation (TransYouthEquality.org /for-parents): advocacy for trans teen and their parents

Video Out (VideoOut.org): a broad set of videos to help you learn more about LGBTQ+ issues

References

Chapter 1

Barnhart, B. "Social Media Demographics to Inform Your Brand's Strategy in 2021." Sprout Social. March 9, 2021. SproutSocial .com/insights/new-social-media-demographics.

Centers for Disease Control and Prevention. *Youth Risk Behavior Survey.* 2019. CDC.gov/healthyyouth/data/yrbs/pdf /YRBSDataSummaryTrendsReport2019-508.pdf.

Gay and Lesbian Medical Association. *Healthy People 2010: Companion Document for Lesbian, Gay, Bisexual, and Transgender (LGBTQ+) Health.* April 2001. GLMA.org /_data/n_0001/resources/live/HealthyCompanionDoc3.pdf.

Human Rights Campaign Foundation. *2018 LGBTQ+ Youth Report.* 2018. HRC.org/resources/2018-lgbtq-youth-report.

Igartua, Karine J., Kathryn Gill, and Richard Montoro. "Internalized Homophobia: A Factor in Depression, Anxiety, and Suicide in the Gay and Lesbian Population." *Canadian Journal of Community Mental Health* 22, no. 2 (2003):15–30. DOI: 10.7870 /cjcmh-2003-0011.

Kliff, Sarah, Soo Oh, and Sarah Frostenson. "Today's Teenagers [blank] Less Than You Did." *Vox.* June 9, 2016. Vox.com/a /teens#year/1997.

LaSala, Michael C. "Lesbians, Gay Men, and Their Parents: Family Therapy for the Coming-Out Crisis." *Family Process* 39, no. 1 (March 2000): 67–81. DOI: 10.1111/j.1545-5300.2000.39108.x.

Morin, Amy. "The Top 10 Social Issues Teens Struggle with Today." Verywell Family. June 24, 2020. VerywellFamily.com /startling-facts-about-todays-teenagers-2608914.

Pew Research Center. "Chapter 3: The Coming Out Experience." *A Survey of LGBTQ+ Americans.* June 13, 2013. PewResearch .org/social-trends/2013/06/13/chapter-3-the-coming -out-experience.

Portnoy, Dennis. "Discovering Your Intrinsic Self." *Unity Magazine.* March 2018. Unity.org/publications/unity-magazine/articles /discovering-your-intrinsic-self.

Rosario, Margaret, Joyce Hunter, Shira Maguen, Marya Gwadz, and Raymond Smith. "The Coming-Out Process and Its Adaptational and Health-Related Associations among Gay, Lesbian, and Bisexual Youths: Stipulation and Exploration of a Model." *American Journal of Community Psychology* 29, no. 1 (February 2001):133–60. DOI: 10.1023/a:1005205630978.

Rothman, Emily F., Mairead Sullivan, Susan Keyes, and Ulrike Boehmer. "Parents' Supportive Reactions to Sexual Orientation Disclosure Associated with Better Health: Results from a Population-Based Survey of LGB Adults in Massachusetts." *Journal of Homosexuality* 59, no. 2 (2012): 186–200. DOI: 10.1080/00918369.2012.648878.

Sears, Andrew. "Are the Kids Alright? Smartphones, Social Media, and Teen Wellbeing." All Tech Is Human. January 25, 2020. AllTechIsHuman.org/blog/are-the-kids-alright -smartphones-social-media-and-teen-wellbeing.

The Pew Charitable Trust. Living Facts. 2020, December 9. LivingFacts.org/en/articles/2020/meet-gen-z.

Chapter 2

Ehrenhalt, Jey. "Being There for Nonbinary Youth." *Learning for Justice, Summer 2016.* LearningForJustice.org/magazine /summer-2016/being-there-for-nonbinary-youth.

Gender Wiki. "Genderqueer." Accessed March 28, 2021. Gender. Wikia.org/wiki/Genderqueer.

Kann, Laura, Emily O'Malley Olsen, Tim McManus, Steve Kinchen, David Chyen, William A. Harris, Howell Wechsler. "Sexual Identity, Sex of Sexual Contacts, and Health-Risk Behaviors among Students in Grades 9–12." *Youth Risk Behavior Surveillance, Selected Sites, United States, 2001–2009*. CDC Surveillance Summaries. *Morbidity and Mortality Weekly Report* (June 10, 2011): 1–133.

LaSala Michael C. "Gay Male Couples: The Importance of Coming Out and Being Out to Parents." *Journal of Homosexuality* 39, no. 2 (2000): 47–71. DOI: 10.1300/J082v39n02_03.

Mills-Koonce, W. Roger, Peter D. Rehder, and Amy L. McCurdy. "The Significance of Parenting and Parent-Child Relationships for Sexual and Gender Minority Adolescents." *Journal of Research on Adolescence* 28, no. 3 (September 2018): 637–49. DOI: 10.1111/jora.12404.

Morin, Amy. "4 Types of Parenting Styles and Their Effects on Kids." Verywell Family. July 12, 2019. VerywellFamily.com/types-of-parenting-styles-1095045#uninvolved-parenting.

Ortiz, Melanie. "The Evolutionary Science Behind Gender." The Metric. June 24, 2020. TheMetric.org/articles/the-evolutionary-science-behind-gender.

Watson, Josh. "Why Is Teen Identity Development Important?" Aspiro. December 11, 2019. AspiroAdventure.com/blog/why-is-teen-identity-development-important.

Chapter 3

American Psychological Association. "Resilience for Teens: Got Bounce?" Updated June 1, 2020. APA.org/topics/resilience/bounce-teens.

Baptist, Joyce A., and Katherine R. Allen. "A Family's Coming-Out Process: Systemic Change and Multiple Realities." *Contemporary Family Therapy* 30, no. 2 (2008): 92–110.

Gonzalez, Kristen A., Sharon S. Rostosky, Robert D. Odom, and Ellen D. B. Riggle. "The Positive Aspects of Being the Parent of an LGBTQ+ Child." *Family Process* 52, no. 2 (June 2013): 325–37. DOI:10.1111/famp.12009.

Goodrich, Kristopher M. "Mom and Dad Come Out: The Process of Identifying as a Heterosexual Parent with a Lesbian, Gay, or Bisexual Child." *Journal of LGBTQ+ Issues in Counseling* 3, no. 1 (2009): 37–61. DOI: 10.1080/15538600902754478.

LaSala, Michael C. *Coming Out, Coming Home: Helping Families Adjust to a Gay or Lesbian Child.* New York: Columbia University Press, 2010.

Luvmour, Josette. "Developing Together: Parents Meeting Children's Developmental Imperatives." *Journal of Adult Development* 18 (2011): 164–71. DOI: 10.1007/s10804 -010-9111-x.

Price-Mitchell, Marylin. "How Role Models Influence Youth Strategies for Success." Roots of Action. November 14, 2020. RootsOfAction.com/role-models-youth-strategies-success.

Radun, Lori. "Family Leadership: Becoming a Successful and Effective Parent Leader." The Momiverse. March 20, 2020. TheMomiverse.com/motherhood-and-family/family -leadership-becoming-a-successful-and-effective -parent-leader.

Chapter 4

American Academy of Child & Adolescent Psychiatry. "Self-Injury in Adolescents." January 2019. AACAP.org/AACAP/Families _and_Youth/Facts_for_Families/FFF-Guide/Self-Injury-In -Adolescents-073.aspx.

Baptist, Joyce A., and Katherine R. Allen. "A Family's Coming-Out Process: Systemic Change and Multiple Realities." *Contemporary Family Therapy* 30, no. 2 (2008): 92–110.

Centers for Disease Control and Prevention. "Sexual Identity,
Sex of Sexual Contacts, and Health-Risk Behaviors among
Students in Grades 9–12: Youth Risk Behavior Surveillance."
Atlanta, GA: U.S. Department of Health and Human Ser-
vices, 2016.

Feinstein, Brian A., Matthew Thomann, Ryan Coventry, Kathryn
Macapagal, Brian Mustanski, and Michael E. Newcomb.
"Gay and Bisexual Adolescent Boys' Perspectives on
Parent-Adolescent Relationships and Parenting Practices
Related to Teen Sex and Dating." *Archives of Sexual Behavior*
47 (2018): 1825–37. DOI:10.1007/s10508-017-1057-7.

Human Rights Campaign Foundation. *Preventing Substance
Abuse among LGBTQ+ Teens*. n.d. Accessed April 15, 2021.
HRC.org/resources/preventing-substance-abuse-among
-lgbtq-teens.

Juergens, Jeffrey. "The LGTBQ Community and Addiction." Addiction Center. Accessed April 15, 2021. AddictionCenter.com
/addiction/lgbtq.

Levy, Gabrielle. "LGBTQ+ Teens Feel Unsafe and Unwelcome,
Despite Growing Support for Rights." *U.S. News & World
Report*. May 15, 2018. USNews.com/news/national-news
/articles/2018-05-15/lgbtq-teens-feel-unsafe-and
-unwelcome-despite-growing-support-for-rights.

Liu, Richard T. "Temporal Trends in the Prevalence of Nonsuicidal
Self-injury among Sexual Minority and Heterosexual Youth
from 2005 through 2017." *JAMA Pediatrics* 173, no. 8 (2019):
790–91. DOI: 10.1001/jamapediatrics.2019.1433.

Mozes, Alan. "Too Often, Bullying Has Lethal Consequences for
LGBTQ+ Teens." *U.S. News & World Report*. May 26, 2020.
USNews.com/news/health-news/articles/2020-05-26
/too-often-bullying-has-lethal-consequences-for-lgbt-teens.

Pappas, Stephanie. "Teaching Porn Literacy." *Monitor on Psychology* 52, no. 2 (March 1, 2021): 54. APA.org/monitor/2021/03/teaching-porn-literacy.

Reddy, Nethan, Callie Silver, and Janis Whitlock. *The Relationship between NSSI and LGBTQ+ Identities*. Ithaca, NY: Cornell Research Program on Self-Injury and Recovery, 2016.

Russell, S. T., B. T. Franz, and A. K. Driscoll. "Same-Sex Romantic Attraction and Experiences of Violence in Adolescence." *American Journal of Public Health* 91, no. 6 (2001): 903–6.

Ryan, Caitlin, and Donna Futterman. "Experiences, Vulnerabilities and Risks" in *Lesbian and Gay Youth: Care and Counseling*, 24–5. New York: Columbia University Press, 1998.

Savin-Williams, Ritch C., and Kenneth M. Cohen. "Ethnic and Sexual-Minority Youth." In *The Lives of Lesbians, Gays, and Bisexuals: Children to Adults*, eds. Ritch C. Savin-Williams and Kenneth M. Cohen, 152–65. Fort Worth: Harcourt Brace College Publishing, 1996.

Thornton, Vanessa. "Eating Disorders in the LGBTQ+ Population." *Today's Dietitian* 20, no. 9 (September 2018): 46–51.

Turban, Jack. "What Is Gender Dysphoria?" American Pyschiatric Association. November 2020. Psychiatry.org/patients-families/gender-dysphoria/what-is-gender-dysphoria.

Williams, A. Jess, Jon Arcelus, Ellen Townsend, and Maria Michail. "Examining Risk Factors for Self-Harm and Suicide in LGBTQ+ Young People: A Systematic Review Protocol." *BMJ Open* 9, no. 11 (2019). DOI: 10.1136/bmjopen-2019-031541.

Chapter 5

Fabien-Weber, Nicole. "20 Questions for Getting to Know Your Teenager." Care.com. April 3, 2019. Care.com/c/stories/778/100-questions-to-get-to-know-your-teenager.

Glicksman, Eve. "R-E-S-P-E-C-T." *Monitor on Psychology* 43, no. 11 (December 2012): 32. APA.org/monitor/2012/12/respect.

Human Rights Campaign Foundation. *2018 LGBTQ+ Youth Report.* n.d. Accessed March 20, 2021. HRC.org/resources/2018 -lgbtq-youth-report.

Lytle, M. C., M. D. Vaughan, E. M. Rodriguez, and D. L. Shmerler. "Working with LGBTQ+ Individuals: Incorporating Positive Psychology into Training and Practice." *Psychology of Sexual Orientation and Gender Diversity* 1, no. 4 (2014): 335–47. DOI: 10.1037/sgd0000064.

Offer, Shira. "Family Time Activities and Adolescents' Emotional Well-being." *Journal of Marriage and Family* 75, no. 1 (February 2013): 26–41. DOI: 10.1111/j.1741-3737.2012.01025.x.

Park, Nansook, and Christopher Peterson. "Moral Competence and Character Strengths among Adolescents: The Development and Validation of the Values in Action Inventory of Strengths for Youth." *Journal of Adolescence* 29, no. 6 (2006): 891–909.

Penn State. "Time with Parents Is Important for Teens' Well-Being." ScienceDaily. August 21, 2012. ScienceDaily.com/releases/2012/08/120821143907.htm.

RaisingChildren.net.au. "Discipline Strategies for Teenagers." Updated October 1, 2019. RaisingChildren.net.au/pre-teens/behaviour/behaviour-management-ideas/discipline.

Remen, Rachel Naomi. Inspiring Quotes. InspiringQuotes.us /author/1040-rachel-naomi-remen.

TCMEDIA. "LGBTQ+ Respect: Be an Ally!" Teencentral. April 10, 2017. TeenCentral.com/lgbtq-respect-be-an-ally.

Chapter 6

DeLoreto, Caroline. "7 Tips for Parents to Help Their Teen Create a Strong Sense of Self." PsychAlive. Accessed April 24, 2021. PsychAlive.org/7-tips-for-parents-to-help-teen-create-strong-sense-of-self.

Jack, Claire. "3 Steps Towards Improving Your Self-Esteem." *Psychology Today*. April 28, 2020. PsychologyToday.com/us/blog/women-autism-spectrum-disorder/202004/3-steps-towards-improving-your-self-esteem.

Kuvalanka, Katherine A., Samuel H. Allen, Cat Munroe, Abbie E. Goldberg, and Judith L. Weiner. "The Experiences of Sexual Minority Mothers with Trans* Children." *Family Relations* 67, no. 1 (February 2018): 70–87. DOI: 10.1111/fare.12226.

Pickhardt, Carl E. "Identity Experimentation in Early and Mid Adolescence." *Psychology Today*. July 11, 2016. PsychologyToday.com/us/blog/surviving-your-childs-adolescence/201607/identity-experimentation-in-early-and-mid-adolescence.

RaisingChildren.net.au. "Discipline Strategies for Teenagers." Updated October 1, 2019. RaisingChildren.net.au/pre-teens/behaviour/behaviour-management-ideas/discipline.

ReachOut.com. "Supportive Parenting and Teenagers." Accessed April 24, 2021. Parents.au.ReachOut.com/skills-to-build/connecting-and-communicating/supportive-parenting-and-teenagers.

Chapter 7

Gomillion, Sarah C., and Traci A. Giuliano. "The Influence of Media Role Models on Gay, Lesbian, and Bisexual Identity." *Journal of Homosexuality* 58, no. 3 (2011): 330–54. DOI: 10.1080/00918369.2011.546729.

Height, Dorothy. AZ Quotes. AZQuotes.com/quote/774454?ref=coming-together.

Index

V

Validation, 53
Values, 58–60, 104
Violence, 102–103
Vulnerability, 97

W

Weil, Andrew, 34
Wooden, John, 108

Acknowledgments

I would like to express appreciation for the Callisto Media team who took a chance on a neophyte writer. It is because of everyone's guidance, patience, and support, from beginning to end, this book was possible.

I would like to thank San Do for his encouragement and support.

I would like to thank my sister, Ann Lall. It is because of your lifelong love, acceptance, and support that I found confidence to author a book.

I would like to thank Jocelyn Pijpaert, who believed in me and encouraged me through moments of insecurity.

I would like to thank Dr. Carlos Parra, who cheered me on throughout this journey.

I would like to thank Carlos Figueroa and Mary Ann Wong, who gave me moments of humor and friendship when I needed it.

About the Author

 **Allan Sadac, MBA, LMFT,** is an LGBTQ+ licensed marriage and family therapist in private practice in Los Alamitos, California. He graduated from UC Davis, majoring in psychology with a minor in human development. He also has a master's degree in counseling. Early in his career, he volunteered at the Sacramento AIDS Foundation and the Sacramento LGBTQ+ Center. Through his work in community mental health, he has helped children, teens, and families identify areas of personal growth and find confidence in creating their own solutions to their unique life challenges. Currently, he continues to find purpose in his clinical work by focusing on the mental health needs of the LGBTQ+ community.